# NUTRITION & HEALTH

# Vegetarianism

## SUSAN M. TRAUGH

**LUCENT BOOKS**

*A part of Gale, Cengage Learning*

**GALE**
CENGAGE Learning™

Detroit • New York • San Francisco • New Haven, Conn • Waterville, Maine • London

**LIBRARY OF CONGRESS CATALOGING-IN-PUBLICATION DATA**

Traugh, Susan M.
Vegetarianism / by Susan M. Traugh.
  p. cm. -- (Nutrition and health)
Includes bibliographical references and index.
ISBN 978-1-4205-0272-5 (hardcover)
1. Vegetarianism. I. Title.
TX392.T725 2011
641.5'636--dc22

2010014015

Lucent Books
27500 Drake Rd.
Farmington Hills, MI 48331

ISBN-13: 978-1-4205-0272-5
ISBN-10: 1-4205-0272-7

Printed in the United States of America
1 2 3 4 5 6 7 14 13 12 11 10

Printed by Bang Printing, Brainerd, MN, 1st Ptg., 08/2010

# TABLE OF CONTENTS

Many people today are often amazed by the amount of nutrition and health information, often contradictory, that can be found in the media. Television, newspapers, and magazines bombard readers with the latest news and recommendations. Television news programs report on recent scientific studies. The healthy living sections of newspapers and magazines offer information and advice. In addition, electronic media such as Web sites, blogs, and forums post daily nutrition and health news and recommendations.

This constant stream of information can be confusing. The science behind nutrition and health is constantly evolving. Current research often leads to new ideas and insights. Many times, the latest nutrition studies and health recommendations contradict previous studies or traditional health advice. When the media report these changes without giving context or explanations, consumers become confused. In a survey by the National Health Council, for example, 68 percent of participants agreed that "when reporting medical and health news, the media often contradict themselves, so I don't know what to believe." In addition, the Food Marketing Institute reported that eight out of ten consumers thought it was likely that nutrition and health experts would have a completely different idea about what foods are healthy within five years. With so much contradictory information, people have difficulty deciding how to apply nutrition and health recommendations to their lives. Students find it difficult to find relevant yet clear and credible information for reports.

Changing recommendations for antioxidant supplements are an example of how confusion can arise. In the 1990s antioxidants such as vitamins C and E and beta-carotene came to the public's attention. Scientists found that people who ate more antioxidant-rich foods had a lower risk of heart disease, cancer, vision loss, and other chronic conditions than those who ate lower amounts. Without waiting for more scientific study, the media and supplement companies quickly spread the word that antioxidants could help fight and prevent disease. They recommended that people take antioxidant supplements and eat fortified foods. When further scientific studies were completed, however, most did not support the initial recommendations. While naturally occurring antioxidants in fruits and vegetables may help prevent a variety of chronic diseases, little scientific evidence proved antioxidant supplements had the same effect. In fact, a study published in the November 2008 *Journal of the American Medical Association* found that supplemental vitamins A and C gave no more heart protection than a placebo. The study's results contradicted the widely publicized recommendation, leading to consumer confusion. This example highlights the importance of context for evaluating nutrition and health news. Understanding a topic's scientific background, interpreting a study's findings, and evaluating news sources are critical skills that help reduce confusion.

Lucent's Nutrition and Health series is designed to help young people sift through the mountain of confusing facts, opinions, and recommendations. Each book contains the most up-to-date information, synthesized and written so that students can understand and think critically about nutrition and health issues. Each volume of the series provides a balanced overview of today's hot-button nutrition and health issues while presenting the latest scientific findings and a discussion of issues surrounding the topic. The series provides young people with tools for evaluating conflicting and ever-changing ideas about nutrition and health. Clear narrative peppered with personal anecdotes, fully documented primary and secondary source quotes, informative sidebars, fact boxes, and statistics are all used to help readers understand these topics and how they affect their bodies and their lives. Each volume includes information about changes in trends over time, political controversies, and international perspectives. Full-color photographs and charts enhance all volumes in the series. The Nutrition and Health series is a valuable resource for young people to understand current topics and make informed choices for themselves.

# Going Greens

More Americans are changing the way they eat and are turning to their "greens." This means including more fruit and vegetables in their diet. Some people have chosen to become vegetarians—they do not eat meat at all. As many as 8 million American adults are vegetarians, according to a 2009 poll conducted by Harris Interactive. A 2002 poll by *Time* magazine indicates that another 20 million have considered adopting some of the eating patterns of vegetarians. Why are so many Americans "going greens"?

A desire to develop a healthier lifestyle is a big reason for this change. Researchers have spent decades studying the nutritional benefits of vegetarianism. Their findings have pointed to a clear conclusion: A plant-based diet is a key factor in improving overall health. Such a diet can help ward off obesity, diabetes, heart disease, high cholesterol, and numerous cancers. It may also help to keep extra weight off and increase longevity.

Those findings are important, as many of these diseases are on the rise, especially in the United States. Other research shows that a simple diet change—away from saturated fat and calories and toward more fruits and vegetables—can dramatically lower Americans' risk factors for certain diseases. With so much evidence at their fingertips, more people are trying to incorporate healthy choices into their eating habits.

## Choosing Vegetarianism for Ethical Reasons

Vegetarianism has a long and varied history dating back to ancient times. Throughout history certain groups of people have shunned eating meat for philosophical or religious reasons. People in ancient India and Greece followed a vegetarian diet as part of their belief in nonviolence toward all living things. Indians, Buddhists, and Hindus advocated vegetarianism because of a belief in the sacredness of all living creatures. The Hindu belief in reincarnation—the return of a human soul into the body of an animal—contributed to the desire to avoid eating the flesh of any creature.

*A Hindu priest offers vegetarian dishes as a form of prayer to the idols of Lord Krishna. Hindus advocate vegetarianism for religious reasons.*

During the time of the Roman Empire (around 27 B.C. to A.D. 476), vegetarianism was not widespread in Europe. But it began to gain favor centuries later as certain religious groups embraced it during the Renaissance, which began in the fourteenth century and lasted until the seventeenth century. In America small groups of people in the 1700s practiced vegetarianism—most notable among them Benjamin Franklin. Although later in life Franklin returned to eating meat, other Americans persisted with their vegetarian practice. Most American vegetarians in the eighteenth and nineteenth centuries belonged to various religious groups that advocated a meat-free diet because they considered the way in which animals were slaughtered to be inhumane. These groups included the Ephrata Cloister, the Bible-Christian Church, the Grahamites, and the Seventh-Day Adventist Church. Today most Seventh-Day Adventists continue to follow a vegetarian diet.

Vegetarianism gained more widespread recognition in Europe and the United States in 1847 with the formation of the Vegetarian Society in England. This society was formed by a group of Christians opposed to eating animal flesh on the grounds that it constituted animal cruelty. The society, which advocated a "live and let live" philosophy toward all creatures and even promoted alternatives to leather shoes, soon spread to other parts of Europe. Then in 1908 the vegetarian diet gained worldwide popularity when the International Vegetarian Union was founded in Germany. Like the Vegetarian Society before it, the International Vegetarian Union advocated abstaining from eating meat for moral reasons. This century-old organization still operates today, bringing together people from all over the world to promote vegetarianism.

Just as people have done throughout history, today people are choosing vegetarianism for a variety of reasons, including religious, moral, nutritional, and philosophical concerns. Whether the change in the way they eat incorporates a fully vegetarian diet or simply involves increased consumption of fruits and vegetables, people today are going for their greens.

# CHAPTER 1

# A Growing Trend

Elisabeth and a group of fellow college students stood outside a theater discussing where to eat after the movie. Burgers and fries were not on the menu for these young people. Elisabeth wanted tofu stir-fry. Paul wanted a cheese pizza. Tanya thought a salad would be nice. Although they all wanted different foods to eat, the thing these young people had in common was that they were all vegetarians.

Today, increasing numbers of people are embracing vegetarianism. In addition to true vegetarians, a much larger group is reducing meat consumption and eating meatless meals on a more regular basis. A growing number of people do not identify themselves as vegetarian but nevertheless occasionally eat vegetarian meals. Vegetarianism is definitely a trend that has grown in popularity in recent years, both in the United States and around the world.

## Managing Weight

As obesity rates have risen in the United States, some people have turned to a vegetarian diet in the belief that it can help keep the pounds off. "I got tired of being fat and always watching what I ate," said fourteen-year-old Sydney.

# Vegetarian Valentine

What makes a vegetarian attractive? People for the Ethical Treatment of Animals (PETA) asked that question when they sponsored the Sexiest Vegetarian over Fifty Contest in 2009. PETA decided that Mimi Kirk, age seventy, deserved the title for women.

A vegetarian since she was thirty, Kirk says: "I stopped eating meat because of the animal killing. I became sensitive to that—to their pain. Now my motto is: Nothing with a face—nothing with a mother!"

Looking healthy, vibrant, and much younger than her seventy years, Kirk travels the globe with her boyfriend. Along the way she speaks out for animal care, planet care, and self-care. Kirk says:

> Everyone needs to do their part and be conscious of the environment and new ways to help the planet. People say it's the president's job—it's ours. We need to take moves ourselves. If young people knew where their meat comes from . . . how those animals are tortured . . . they could not be blind to that death. If you don't feel for the animals, then feel for the planet—or, at least, think of your own health.

Mimi Kirk, interview with the author, August 25, 2009.

"A couple of my mom's friends were vegetarians and they ate whatever they wanted and looked great. So, I tried it and it worked for me."[1]

Research supports Sydney's choice. A large number of scientific studies have focused on veganism, the most extreme of the vegetarian diets. Vegans avoid all food products that come from animals, including foods such as eggs and honey. Only about 1.5 percent of the population follows this diet. Yet the vegan diet seems to offer clear health benefits.

One example of this can be seen in a 2009 study conducted at Loma Linda University. There, researchers studied the eating habits of 60,900 people. They found that vegans had half the risk of diabetes compared to nonvegetarians. One of the reasons for their lower risk was their lower weights. As a group the vegans were significantly thinner than the meat eaters.

Other research has supported these findings. In 2006 Susan E. Berkow and Neal Barnard of the Physicians Committee for Responsible Medicine, a nonprofit group of doctors that completes independent research, reviewed eighty-seven previous studies on veganism and vegetarianism. Their analysis showed that a low-fat vegan diet led to a weight loss of about a pound (0.45kg) a week without additional exercise or limits on portions. Berkow explains the benefits of adding more fruit and vegetables to the diet: "Our research reveals that people can enjoy unlimited portions of high-fiber foods such as fruits, vegetables and whole grains to achieve or maintain a healthy body weight without feeling hungry."[2]

Some concrete studies have shown that a vegetarian diet is also related to maintaining a healthy weight. In their analysis of past studies, Berkow and Barnard found that only about 6 percent of vegetarians were overweight, while up to 45 percent of nonvegetarians were. They report that "vegetarians were less likely to be obese and that vegetarian diets brought greater weight loss."[3] In several of the studies Berkow and Barnard reviewed, researchers had attempted to control for other healthy lifestyle factors. Were vegetarians thinner because they practiced a healthier lifestyle overall, or was the diet the main factor in weight control? By controlling for exercise, alcohol consumption, and other factors, researchers believe they were able to point to diet as a significant factor in weight control.

Not only do vegetarians lose weight, but they keep it off. In a five-year study, physician Dean Ornish found that overweight people following a low-fat vegetarian diet lost an average of 24 pounds (11kg) the first year and still kept the weight off five years later. They did not count calories nor measure portions, but instead just stayed on a whole-foods diet.

# How Many U.S. Vegetarians Are There?

Elisabeth and Sydney are part of a growing number of people in the United States who are turning to a vegetarian diet. In a 2009 survey from the Vegetarian Resource Group conducted by Harris Interactive, 8 percent of Americans reported they never ate meat. Based on these data, an estimated 6 to 8 million adults in the United States consider themselves to be vegetarians.

But an interesting trend becomes apparent upon further examination. A 2003 Harris Interactive survey found that 10 percent of twenty-five- to thirty-four-year-olds never eat meat. This number has remained consistent as that group of young people has traveled through the age groups from their teenaged years, leading some analysts to speculate that vegetarianism among younger people is both pervasive and permanent. And young people may have compelling reasons to choose and to stick with a vegetarian diet, according to the KidsHealth Web site: "Preteens and teens often voice their independence through the foods they choose to eat. One strong statement is the decision to stop eating meat. This is common among teens, who may decide to embrace vegetarianism in support of animal rights, for health reasons, or because friends are doing it."[4]

Of those people who define themselves as vegetarian, the Vegetarian Resource Group estimates that between one-third and one-half are vegans. Surprised by the high percentage of vegans in its survey, the group looked back at its data over the years and found a consistent pattern. The group said, "This number may seem too high, but our theory is that most people who fit the definition of vegetarian (never eat meat, fish, or fowl) are 'very committed to issues' and tend to become vegan."[5]

In addition to the true vegetarians, a growing number of people occasionally seek out meat-free meals. Charles Stahler, codirector of the Vegetarian Resource Group, estimates that about 30 to 40 percent of Americans at least occasionally eat vegetarian meals. Most do so for the health benefits shown to come from consuming less meat.

It does appear that vegetarianism is growing among all Americans. The trend also seems to be growing especially quickly among the young people.

## Who Becomes a Vegetarian?

Elisabeth represents the typical vegetarian. She is young, female, a student, and living in California. Harris Interactive fielded a recent survey for the Vegetarian Resource Group to determine what types of people become vegetarian. They interviewed 2,397 U.S. adults nationwide and weighted the results based on region, gender, age, education, household income, race/ethnicity, and propensity to be online.

The survey found that people who consider themselves vegetarians come from all categories of American life. Students are the largest group, with 15 percent of high school and college students defining themselves as vegetarian. More females than males follow a vegetarian diet. The East and

*Students compose the largest group of vegetarians, with 15 percent of high school and college students defining themselves as such.*

West coasts also boast a larger percentage of vegetarians than the country's heartland.

Another group that includes a high percentage of vegetarians is those who dine out. A 2008 Zogby poll of Americans showed that more than 40 percent are choosing meatless meals at least part of the time when they eat out. This percentage includes fairly equal numbers of Republicans and Democrats as well as those defining themselves as "very" conservative and "very" liberal. People of all ethnicities and religious backgrounds enjoy vegetarian meals when dining out.

Steven, a teacher and father of three, is one of those diners who usually orders vegetarian meals when he goes out. He says: "I do eat meat, although not as often as I used to. . . . When I'm out, I like to get something that feels healthy and special. Whether it's spicy eggplant or a really exotic salad, I enjoy ordering dishes that I couldn't or wouldn't make at home."[6]

## All Vegetarian Diets Are Not the Same

Vegetarians are not one defined group of people, but rather come from all walks of life. Similarly, no single vegetarian diet exists. Instead, vegetarianism includes many different eating philosophies. A vegetarian diet can include four options:

> **Lacto-ovo vegetarian**: *Lacto* means "milk." *Ovo* means "egg." This group eats a plant-based diet plus dairy products and eggs, but does not eat meat, fish, or fowl.
>
> **Lacto vegetarian**: This group eats a plant-based diet and adds dairy products to that diet. They do not eat eggs, meat, fish, or fowl.
>
> **Ovo vegetarian**: This group supplements a plant-based diet with eggs but does not eat dairy, meat, fish, or fowl.
>
> **Vegan**: This is the strictest vegetarian group. They eat only plant-based foods and shun all animal products, including meat, fish, fowl, dairy, eggs, and honey. In addition, vegans do not use any animal products, such as leather, wool, or silk.

Today, popular culture is altering the classic definition of *vegetarianism*. Flexitarians are people who *mostly* eat vegetarian. Semi-vegetarians do not eat red meat. Pesco-vegetarians, or pescotarians, do not eat meat or poultry but do eat fish. Pollo-vegetarians, or pollotarians, do not eat meat or fish but do eat poultry. Although not technically vegetarians, these people nevertheless may define themselves as vegetarians.

Others may simply engage in wishful thinking when defining themselves as vegetarians. Richard Corliss reports in *Time* magazine that in a survey of eleven thousand people, 37 percent of those who described themselves as vegetarian also reported eating red meat within the twenty-four hours before the survey. Sixty percent stated they had eaten either red meat, fish, or poultry in the past day. Christy Pugh, a bookkeeper from New Hampshire, is one example of a meat-eating vegetarian. Although she usually follows a vegetarian diet, her meals sometimes include one of her favorite foods: organic turkey sausage.

*Vegetarian Times* magazine is the standard-bearer of the vegetarian movement. The organization is clear about its stand on so-called vegetarians who eat meat: "For many people who are working to become vegetarians, chicken and fish may be transitional foods, but they are not vegetarian foods . . . the word 'vegetarian' means someone who eats no meat, fish or chicken."[7] But Pugh explained her reasons for occasionally consuming meat: "Sometimes I feel like I'm a bad vegetarian, that I'm not strict enough or good enough. I really like vegetarian food but I'm just not 100 percent committed."[8] Suzanne Havala Hobbs, a nutrition professor at the University of North Carolina at Chapel Hill, adds: "Whether you make a commitment to eating strictly vegetarian or not, cutting back your dependence on meat is something most people acknowledge they know they should do."[9]

## NUTRITION FACT

### Fruitarians

People who eat only the parts of a plant that can be easily replaced, such as fruit, berries, nuts and tomatoes.

Whether they are true vegetarians or only partial vegetarians who occasionally consume meat or poultry, teens and adults all across America are changing the way they eat. And these health-conscious changes are being reflected in the marketplace.

## The Changing Face of Food

Vegetarians are bringing their food preferences to their local eateries and grocers. Thirty percent of U.S. consumers make purchasing decisions based on issues concerning the environment, social justice, and health, according to a survey by the Natural Marketing Institute. This group is part of the consumer trend that has fueled the surge in vegetarian fare in grocery stores, as reported in the food industry magazine *Supermarket News*.

A few years ago any fast food restaurant would have been off-limits for a vegetarian because its meat-saturated menu would have provided no choices for people on a plant-based diet. But that is changing, in large part because beef consumption is down in the United States from its high in 1976. Back then, Americans ate about 94 pounds (42.6kg) of beef each year. Now consumption is down to 64 pounds (30.8kg) per person annually. As more and more people move away from eating meat, vegetarian offerings are becoming commonplace in many restaurants all over the country. Burger King, for example, offers a BK Veggie Burger that meets the requirements of a strict vegetarian diet.

The aisles of America's grocery stores are also changing. Vegetarian foods used to occupy a small "health foods" section next to the ethnic foods. Now plant-based meat substitutes and vegetarian-friendly foods are displayed in nearly every aisle. In fact, a 2006 survey on the supermarket conducted for *Supermarket News* reported that vegetarian food sales were expected to continue to increase, bringing in an additional $1.7 billion in revenue over five years. That is a promising increase in an industry that is seeing its sales flatten out or even shrink and one of the few bright spots in an industry hit hard by poor economic times.

Many consumers are pleased by the changes they see in grocery stores. Reed Mangels, a registered dietician and the mother of three teenage vegetarians, is one such individual. She says: "We visit my parents in northern Florida once a year. When we first started going 15 years ago, we'd pack an entire suitcase with soy milk and other foods. Now I don't bring anything. The local grocery chain has a good selection of vegetarian foods, which is significant because it's not a particularly progressive community."[10]

Changes such as these are also good news for vegetarians when they visit a restaurant. "What's nice," contends Elisabeth, "is that I can go to the store or a fast food place with my friends and easily pick up foods that make us all happy. I might have a veggie burger while my boyfriend has a chicken sandwich. It's nice to have that kind of selection."[11]

*Veggie burgers, such as the one shown here, are becoming commonplace in restaurants and grocery stores around the country.*

## Famous Vegetarians, Past and Present

Abraham Lincoln, president

Mohandas Gandhi, Indian leader

George Bernard Shaw, playwright

Henry David Thoreau, writer

Hank Aaron, baseball player

Albert Einstein, scientist

Brad Pitt, actor

Natalie Portman, actor

Alice Walker, poet, writer

Billy Martin, musician

Ellen DeGeneres, TV personality, actor

Tommy Lee, musician

Yasmin Le Bon, supermodel

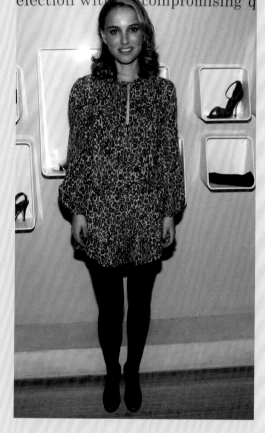

*Actress and vegetarian activist Natalie Portman celebrates the launch of her vegan footwear line in New York City.*

Stahler of the Vegetarian Resource Group believes the driving force behind the move toward vegetarian options at fast food restaurants is due to the growing number of flexitarians and nonvegetarians who desire to eat vegetarian foods on occasion. Stahler says: "This is why Burger King has a veggie burger. It's not because of [vegetarians]. The true vegetarians wouldn't rush to Burger King anyway. It's because of those people in the middle. They are the driving audience."[12]

Veggie burgers and other meat substitutes have become so common that such foods are even included in diabetic diet plans. In the 2003 edition of the American Dietetic Association/American Diabetes Exchange diet, one line was devoted to meat substitutes for people trying to adhere to a low-fat diet to control their diabetes. In 2008 two full pages of plant-based proteins were listed, including veggie bacon and burgers, edamame (soybeans), tempeh (fermented soybeans), hummus (a pureed chickpea spread), soy sausage, and soy-based chicken nuggets.

Whether it is in mainstream diet recommendations, restaurants across the country, or the local supermarket, vegetarian foods are becoming more and more common. And that is good news for vegetarians, nonvegetarians, and everyone in between who wants to consume a meat-free meal.

## Vegetarian Food Producers

The growth in the vegetarian food market has also led to a rise in the number of companies in the food industry that are producing vegetarian foods, including meat, dairy, and egg alternatives. The Vegetarian and Meat-Free Manufacturing Liaison Group reports on its Web site: "Vegetarian and meat-free food sales have boomed over the past decade as the consumption of meat-free products have expanded beyond the highly specialised vegetarian market and been adopted by mainstream consumers."[13] Among the growing number of companies that produce such foods are Linda McCartney Foods, Eden Foods, Imagine Foods, Melissa's/World Variety Produce, Amy's Foods, Food Tech International, and many others. Brand names on boxes in the freezer aisle of local grocery stores also include Boca Burger, Morningstar Farms, Natural Touch, and Loma Linda, among others.

## NUTRITION FACT

**300,000**

Number of people who die each year from diseases related to obesity.

*Vegetarian activists march during a "veggie pride" event in France. The popularization of vegetarianism has more consumers turning to vegetarian choices, if even for an occasional meal.*

The Vegetarian Resource Group describes this explosion in the vegetarian food producing industry as well as the potential for further growth in this market:

From cafeteria lines to restaurant menus to grocery aisles, the range of vegetarian options continues to grow. Greater availability will attract more people to sample these foods. Retaining customers who purchase vegetarian foods occasionally, frequently, or as part of a committed lifestyle requires that offerings meet consumers' primary decision factor for eating: flavor. Great tasting meals that are convenient and reasonably priced will help drive additional expansion of the vegetarian foods market.[14]

## A Growing Trend

Although it is difficult to determine exactly how many true vegetarians there are in America today, the trend is clear: people are increasingly turning to meat-free foods. And this demand for vegetarian food is being met by restaurants, grocers, and food producers alike. It appears that vegetarianism is growing, and even if only for an occasional meal, consumers are embracing vegetarian foods in ever-growing numbers.

# CHAPTER 2

# Why Turn to Vegetarianism?

In her book *The Vegetarian Myth*, Lierre Keith divides the reasons that people choose vegetarianism into three major themes: nutritional, political, and moral. Each of these groups has very different philosophies about why they eat the way they do.

## Nutritional Vegetarians

Nutritional vegetarians believe that their diet contains health benefits. These people want to control their weight, ward off cancer and diabetes, prevent heart disease, or regulate high blood pressure.

## Controlling Cardiovascular Disease

Until 2008 cardiovascular disease was the leading cause of death in the United States, killing more than 800,000 people annually. According to the American Heart Association, 80 million people had one or more forms of cardiovascular disease in 2006. Of those people killed by cardiovascular disease, nearly 151,000 of them were under sixty-five years old.

A significant number of studies show that a low-fat vegetarian diet can reduce heart disease by lowering cholesterol. Lowered cholesterol levels can have a major effect on the health of the heart. The Internet Health Library reported in 2006 that a reduction of 10 percent in blood cholesterol may lead to as much as a 30 percent reduction in the incidence of heart disease.

The human body needs cholesterol to function properly. Cholesterol is a waxy substance that is made in the liver and also obtained from food. Each cell membrane of the human body contains cholesterol and could not function properly without it. Cholesterol also helps digest fats.

*Low-fat vegetarian diets can help reduce cholesterol, which lowers the risk of cardiovascular disease.*

The problem arises when too much cholesterol circulates through the blood and starts to deposit itself on the walls of arteries. That waxy texture allows it to stick together and form a substance called plaque. As plaque builds up, it narrows the passageway for blood flow. Eventually, it can completely block an artery, causing either a heart attack or stroke, depending on where that block is located.

Changes in diet can affect the body's production of cholesterol. A diet high in fiber and low in fat has been found to reduce cholesterol levels. Frank, who owns a construction company in Florida, had an elevated cholesterol level. So his doctor suggested a new diet that excluded one of Frank's favorite foods: "He took away my steak!"[15] lamented Frank.

The elimination of red meat is usually one of the first things a doctor will suggest to patients with high cholesterol. The cholesterol and saturated fat in red meat is a troublesome combination. Frank's steak floods his body with its own cholesterol while forcing his liver to produce more cholesterol to digest the saturated fat in the meat.

Red meat seems to be the biggest culprit in raising cholesterol levels, although butter and ice cream are also major contributors. Abstaining from all meat yields dramatic results in heart health. Findings from the twelve-year Oxford Vegetarian Study showed that death from coronary heart disease was 28 percent lower in vegetarians than meat eaters. The study followed thousands of vegetarians and meat eaters who had been matched for other factors such as age and activity level.

## Never Too Young to Start

The benefits of avoiding saturated fat begin early in life. By cutting back on saturated fat, young people can keep their arteries clear and protect their cardiovascular health. The

Coronary Artery Risk Development in Young Adults Study, a twenty-year study, followed five thousand eighteen- to thirty-year-olds and found that vegetarianism was linked to an increase in cardiovascular health and a decrease in the risk of heart disease.

Scientists now know that plaque buildup in arteries begins young. "Most people think of heart disease as an adult disease," says Arthur Zieske, a pathologist at Louisiana State University. "But what we have found is it affects young people—very young people—too."[16]

This situation does not have to happen. Zieske suggests several steps young people can take to keep their arteries clear. He says, "Finding dangerous advanced plaques in teenagers and young adults tells us definitively that if we are to reduce heart attacks and deaths . . . we need to make sure our children are eating healthy foods, exercising and not smoking."[17]

Other steps are also helpful. Ruth Frechman, a registered dietician, is a spokesperson for the American Dietetic Association. She says that although the hazards of cholesterol-raising foods are well known, some "functional foods" can make a big impact on lowering cholesterol levels. Fatty fish, walnuts, oatmeal, oat bran, and foods fortified with plant sterols including butter-substitute spreads, fortified fruit juices and enhanced fiber bars fit this group. She says, "These foods may not be magic, but they're close to it."[18]

How magic? According to WebMD, "The FDA has reviewed the research on each of these foods, and given them the status of a 'health claim' for managing cholesterol."[19] Health claims are only granted when substantial scientific data has revealed the health benefits of a specific product. And except for fish, the other functional foods are major components of a healthy vegetarian diet. This means a vegetarian diet can help manage cholesterol.

People can do a great deal to decrease heart disease by taking charge of their health, whether or not they choose to be vegetarian. But vegetarianism has been shown to provide additional health benefits. Vegetarians the world over are experiencing improved heart health through a plant-based diet and by avoiding red meat.

# The Meat of the Matter

In addition to high cholesterol levels and heart disease, the saturated fat in red meat is a known contributor to diabetes. Each year Americans eat 40 billion burgers, according to Dave Zinezinko and Matt Goulding. In their article "America's Best and Worst Burgers," they say that means each person eats about 150 burgers each year. They point out that one restaurant chain's double cheeseburger contains 116 grams of fat and 52 grams of saturated fat. By comparison, the American Heart Association recommends people limit their fat intake to 50 to 70 grams per day and their saturated fat intake to 16 grams per day. One double cheeseburger, then, provides more than three days' worth of saturated fat. One hundred and fifty burgers a year means the average American eats one every two to three days, so those burgers alone pump up saturated fat levels above recommended amounts.

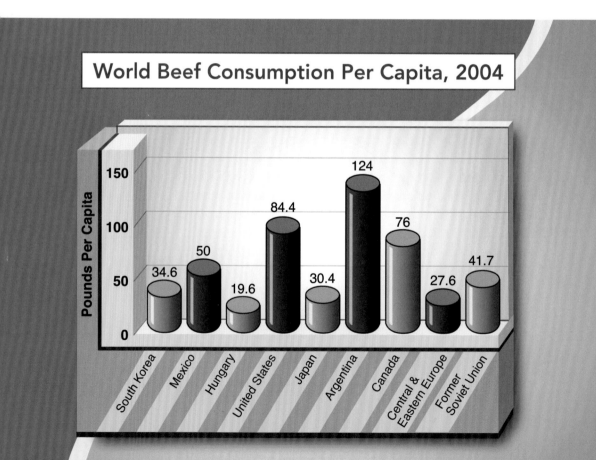

**World Beef Consumption Per Capita, 2004**

Pounds Per Capita

| South Korea | Mexico | Hungary | United States | Japan | Argentina | Canada | Central & Eastern Europe | Former Soviet Union |
|---|---|---|---|---|---|---|---|---|
| 34.6 | 50 | 19.6 | 84.4 | 30.4 | 124 | 76 | 27.6 | 41.7 |

Source: www.cattlerange.com.

A study from the National Institute of Diabetes and Digestive and Kidney Diseases together with the Diabetes Action Research and Education Foundation found a link between meat consumption and diabetes. In this study, they randomly placed diabetics in two groups. One group followed the American Diabetic Association's (ADA) recommended diet—a low-fat, calorie-restricted diet that included low-fat meat consumption. The other group was placed on a low-fat vegan diet. This group did not eat any meat, poultry, fish, dairy, or eggs. Participants were asked not to change their exercise or medication habits.

After twenty-two weeks, both groups had lost weight, but the vegan group had lost more than twice as much as the ADA group. Both groups had also lowered their cholesterol levels. Again, the vegan group's change was nearly double that of the ADA group. In addition, both groups had improved blood lipid (fat) levels and had better blood sugar control.

But as researchers looked further, they found some additional benefits of the vegan diet. Insulin resistance is related to lipid accumulation in the muscle cells. This accumulation triggers a genetic response in some people that decreases their ability to metabolize foods. High-fat diets, especially diets high in saturated fats, seem to impair the genes needed for metabolism. When researchers looked at the ADA group (who were on a low-fat omnivore diet) and the vegans, they found lipid concentration levels were significantly lower in the vegan group as compared to the omnivores.

The researchers' conclusion was that the vegan diet, with its absence of dietary cholesterol, low saturated fat, and specific cholesterol-reducing effect of soluble fiber was not only more effective in controlling diabetes, but "is particularly important given that cardiovascular complications are the primary cause of morbidity and mortality in diabetes."[20]

## Cancer Prevention

In 2008 cancer overtook heart disease as the number one killer of Americans. No matter where it occurs in the body, cancer is a disease of overgrowth. Human cells grow, divide,

## Sustainability

Sustainability is a movement that supports practices that allow the planet to remain diverse and productive over time. In terms of plant-based foods, this requires a change in the common corporate farm.

Corporate farms plant the same crops in neat rows so machinery can harvest and process the crops. The process is efficient for obtaining large amounts of produce. But those neat rows expose precious topsoil, which then blows away. Chemical fertilizers must then be used to replace nutrients exhausted from repeated plantings. Thus, farmland is losing its fertility and produce has substantially fewer nutrients. A study by the European Union discovered that organic produce has 40 percent more antioxidants than commercial produce.

That rich produce is most easily found at local farmers' markets. Farm fresh, often organic, the seasonal fruits and vegetables of the farmer's market are a treat for the eye and tongue alike. By shopping from neighbors, people save fossil fuel, help support sustainable farming methods, and keep money in their communities.

and die off. Cancer cells grow and divide, but then the system goes haywire. Cells continue to grow out of control, often intruding into organs and moving to other parts of the body where they continue their out-of-control growth. In 2008 cancer accounted for approximately 30 percent of annual deaths.

Scientists know that many cancers are lifestyle related. The connection between smoking and lung cancer is one example. But diet is also a leading factor in cancer prevention. The World Cancer Research Fund suggests people can minimize their cancer risk by "reducing the intake of dietary fat and increasing the consumption of fruits, vegetables and whole grains."[21] Kenneth Calman, former chief medical officer of Scotland and England, goes further when he says, "There is a relationship between eating red meat and cancer."[22]

A vegetarian diet also seems to lead to reduced cancer rates. According to William Harris, a physician who produces educational material on vegetarianism, numerous studies have shown that a vegetarian diet reduces the risk for breast cancer, ovarian cancer, prostate cancer, intestinal cancer, lung cancer, and lymphatic cancer. Harris concludes, "There are no logical arguments for the continued use of animal source food in the human diet."[23]

## More Reasons to Try It

Along with avoiding some nutritional pitfalls, nutritional vegetarians believe the diet offers further protections, such as avoiding toxic chemicals. The Environmental Protection Agency (EPA) estimates that nearly 95 percent of pesticide residue in a typical American diet comes from meat, fish, and dairy products. Many vegetarians try to avoid these by limiting their consumption or buying organic dairy products. Buying organic also lets them avoid exposure to steroids and hormones. Candace, a nurse who works with an alternative medicine group, says: "I only buy organic and eat vegetarian because I try to avoid the toxins found in factory-farmed meat and dairy products. Whenever possible, I try to buy from my local organic farmers so I know what I'm getting."[24]

Avoiding the problems associated with spoiled or improperly prepared meat is another benefit of vegetarianism. When Brittney, a high school student, ate an undercooked hamburger at a fast food restaurant, it became the last burger she ever ate. "I was so sick," she says. "I decided that I was never going to put my body through that again and going veg would be the safest thing for me to do. It must have worked because I've never been sick since."[25]

Although it worked for Brittney, vegetarianism does not guarantee food safety. The 2006 E. coli–infected spinach outbreak is proof that food-borne pathogens can affect vegetarians as well. Still, buoyed by EPA findings on pesticides and their knowledge of hormone use in farm animals, vegetarians feel they are taking steps toward avoiding unwanted additions to their food.

*Michael F. Roizen, author of* The Real Age Diet: Make Yourself Younger with What You Eat, *endorses vegetarianism to increase life expectancy.*

Still others want to live longer, healthier lives. Michael F. Roizen is the author of *The Real Age Diet: Make Yourself Younger with What You Eat.* He says, "People who consume saturated, four-legged fat have a shorter life span and more disability at the end of their lives."[26]

Whatever reason they cite, nutritional vegetarians have a large body of evidence to support the health benefits of a vegetarian diet.

## Political Vegetarians

Elisabeth shares many of the beliefs of political vegetarians. She links her choice to be vegetarian with being more environmentally sensitive. She says, "For me, my health and nutrition are no different than the health and nutrition of the planet and the animals that share that planet with me."[27]

For many political vegetarians, their disagreement with the factory farm system in this country and that system's impact on the environment led them to vegetarianism. Most of America's meats are produced by concentrated animal feeding operations, or CAFOs. CAFOs are extraordinarily efficient at producing cheap meat, but environmentalists, animal activists, and other groups are concerned about the hidden costs, both to the life and well-being of the animals and to humans and the planet.

The sheer number of cattle raised for meat consumption is creating an air-pollution problem. A California study found that one dairy cow "emits 19.3 pounds of volatile organic compounds per year, making dairies the largest source of the smog-making gas."[28] Multiply that 19.3 pounds (8.75kg) by the 35 million cattle raised each year and therein lies the problem. In fact, cattle produce more smog-making gases than all America's trucks and passenger cars combined. Those greenhouse gases mix with other pollutants from factory farms, including dust, mold, bacteria, and fungi from cattle feces and feed to create more than 7,000 tons (6,350 metric tons) of particulate pollution in Texas alone.

Factory farms produce enormous amounts of manure, and getting rid of it can be a problem. In a 1997 U.S. Senate report, researchers wrote that livestock produced 130 times as much waste as humans. To dispose of this massive waste, farms spread manure on fields within and around the farm. In smaller

> ## NUTRITION FACT
>
> ### 1
>
> Number of chicken dinners one would have to replace with a vegetarian meal in order to prevent as much carbon dioxide pollution as taking more than 500,000 cars off U.S. roads.

quantities, manure breaks down and is actually good for the soil. But the sheer quantity of manure produced by CAFOs means that farmers must pile the waste in deep layers over the fields. The problem is that deep layers of manure cannot break down into the soil. The runoff from the raw manure pollutes nearby streams and waterways with a potent mix of bacteria, drugs from the food and animal waste, and ammonia from urine that seeps into the groundwater.

One of the most striking results of this practice can be seen in the Gulf of Mexico. Algae blooms from all that waste and fertilizer flowing down the Mississippi are starving out sea animals in the gulf waters, causing a dead zone the size of Maryland.

## Two Sides to the Story

According to author Lierre Keith, political vegetarians follow their diet because they believe it is a just and sustainable way for humans to obtain food. She writes that some vegetarians think the diet is "honorable, ennobling even. Reasons like justice, compassion, a desperate and all-encompassing longing to set the world right. To save the planet. . . . To protect the vulnerable, the voiceless. To feed the hungry. At the very least to refrain from participating in the horror of factory farming."[29]

In many ways vegetarians believe that they are doing their part to save the planet. This kind of talk sets the beef industry and meat eaters on edge. These people believe that a healthy diet can include meat, and they worry that anti-meat campaigns could ruin a major American industry. During a taping of her show in 1995, Oprah Winfrey was told about the practice of feeding processed livestock to cattle, which has been linked to outbreaks of mad cow disease. Upon hearing this, Winfrey said the news "just stopped me cold from eating another burger."[30] Sales of beef plummeted, and the beef industry lost more than $12 million. The beef industry promptly sued her for food defamation.

Food defamation laws are relatively new laws that allow agribusiness to sue any group, journalist, or individual who spreads allegedly false information on the hazards of perishable food. These laws often conflict with freedom of speech and are being contested in court. That is what happened with Winfrey. Ultimately, the beef industry lost the suit. But many of the issues raised during the conflict are worth noting.

According to the Cattlemen's Beef Board Web site, the cattle and beef industry make up the largest segment of U.S. agriculture, representing more than $65 billion in revenue in 2005. Beef industry representatives point out that millions of businesses and hardworking people are affected by a decreased demand for beef. They also contend that much of the land they use is unsuitable for farming and that they provide America's number one source of protein.

*Oprah Winfrey celebrates after the lawsuit filed against her by Texas cattle ranchers was dropped. Ranchers sued Winfrey for allegedly defaming the beef industry in one of her shows.*

As for vegetarianism, Keith points out that it has a downside. She points out: "The truth is that agriculture is the most destructive thing humans have done to the planet, and more of the same won't save us. The truth is that agriculture requires the wholesale destruction of entire ecosystems. The truth is also that life isn't possible without death."[31] Clearly, choosing vegetarianism to reduce harm to the planet requires some careful thought.

## Moral Vegetarians

A third category of vegetarianism is moral vegetarianism. These vegetarians refrain from killing living things. Both the Hindus and Buddhists fall into this category. One well-known moral vegetarian was Indian political leader Mohandas Gandhi. Considered the father of the Indian nation, he was also a Hindu spiritual leader. He described the reasons for his vegetarianism in a 1931 speech at a meeting organized by the London Vegetarian Society:

> Vegetarians should have that moral basis—that a man was not born a carnivorous animal, but born to live on the fruits and herbs that the earth grows. . . . The basis of my vegetarianism is not physical, but moral. If anybody said that I should die if I did not take beef tea or mutton, even on medical advice, I would prefer death. This is the basis of my vegetarianism.[32]

For today's moral vegetarians, it is not just that animals are killed—it is *how* they are killed. Angry at the factory farm system, which they believe is abusing animals, they are demonstrating their displeasure by refraining from eating meat. Unlike political vegetarians, who are concerned about factory farms for the environmental damage that they cause, moral vegetarians care about the killing of any animal for food in general and, specifically, the cruelty they perceive in that killing on factory farms.

Each year 10 billion land animals are raised and killed in factory farms. According to the Humane Society of the United States, "They're mutilated. They're crammed into tiny cages. And they endure often agonizing slaughter."[33] To

# World's Greatest Lifesaver

Although most people have never heard of him, Norman E. Borlaug is credited with saving 1 billion lives—more than anyone in history. He did this by developing high-yield crops such as corn and wheat that helped avert mass starvation.

Born on a farm in Iowa in 1914, Borlaug attended a one-room schoolhouse through the eighth grade. He began his career in the U.S. Forestry Service, then returned to school and received a doctoral degree in plant pathology. Between 1944 and 1960, he focused on increasing wheat production in Mexico. His success earned him the Nobel Peace Prize in 1970 and transformed agriculture. Virtually unknown when he died in 2009, Borlaug is nevertheless credited as the father of the "green revolution," and he helped world food production to more than double between 1960 and 1990.

"Norman E. Borlaug saved more lives than any man in human history," says Josette Sheeran, executive director of the UN World Food Program. "His heart was as big as his brilliant mind, but it was his passion and compassion that moved the world."

Quoted in Matt Curry and Betsy Blaney, "Norman Borlaug Dead," *Huffington Post*, September 13, 2009. www.huffingtonpost.com/2009/09/13/norman-borlaug-dead_n_284886.html.

*Norman E. Borlaug was awarded the Nobel Peace Prize in 1970 for his work developing agriculture in poor countries.*

produce meat quickly, the conveyor belts that process the animals often move too fast for workers to kill all of them adequately before processing. That speed means that many animals suffer excruciating deaths. Workers, too, sometimes suffer. Injuries from perilous working conditions have made slaughterhouse jobs some of the most dangerous in the country.

Vegans, who attempt not to kill any living thing except plants, make up a large portion of moral vegetarians. But Keith counters that it is not possible to live on the planet without killing. Whether it is the plow that destroys the rodent homes in its path or the bone meal that is thrown on the growing vegetables, something must die so something else can live. Either the shrinking supply of fossil fuel fertilizes factory-farmed crops, or traditional fertilizers such as bone meal nourish the food supply. Either way, she contends, there are no free meals.

By removing themselves from meat consumption, moral vegetarians hope to be a factor in ending cruelty to animals. But like the position of the political vegetarian, the moral vegetarian finds no single easy answer.

## The Final Decision

In the end, each person must decide what is right for him- or herself. There are compelling health reasons to abstain from meat consumption and increase fruit and vegetable consumption. But other health-minded people may choose simply to cut back on meat or eat leaner cuts of meat and fish while increasing their fruits, vegetables, and fiber.

# CHAPTER 3

# Nutritionally Speaking

People choose to be vegetarians for as many reasons as there are people. Why they choose to become vegetarians determines how they practice the diet. Some people simply choose to avoid meat. Others forgo all animal products. But whatever path they choose, each group shares the common need for a healthy diet.

## The Food Pyramid

Vegetarian or not, Americans need to watch their portions. "Portion distortion" occurs when Americans lose sight of what a true portion should look like. One-half cup of pasta is a serving—it is one-third cup for a diabetic—yet few Americans would tolerate that small a portion.

Like the standard American diet, the vegetarian diet has a food pyramid. The pyramid provides a visual clue about how to eat. The top, pointed section is the smallest portion and is for the fats, oils, and sweets that are heavy on calories. The pyramid suggests these be used sparingly. In the case of the vegetarian diet, these fats are good fats—but it is still possible to get too much of a good thing. A single serving of fats, oils or sweets would equal one teaspoon of oil or butter, one teaspoon of sugar, one teaspoon of honey, or one tablespoon of mayonnaise or salad dressing.

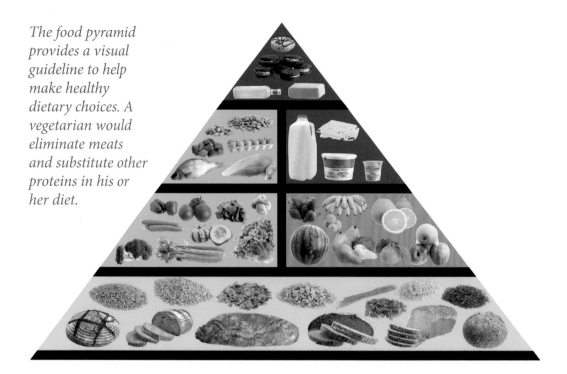

*The food pyramid provides a visual guideline to help make healthy dietary choices. A vegetarian would eliminate meats and substitute other proteins in his or her diet.*

In the next section of the pyramid sit dairy and protein. Dairy is an excellent source of calcium. Both calcium and protein are essential for human health, and 2 to 3 servings of each are recommended each day. A single serving of dairy would include 1 cup of milk or soy milk, 1 cup of yogurt, or 1.5 ounces (45g) of cheese or soy cheese. A single serving of protein would include one-half cup of cooked beans, 4 ounces (115g) of tofu, 1 egg, or 2 tablespoons of nuts, seeds, or peanut butter.

Fruits and vegetables make up the next section. Three to five servings of vegetables are recommended daily. In fact, some nutritionists are now saying Americans should have up to nine servings of vegetables a day. Leafy greens are the vegetable of choice here. A single serving of vegetables would be one cup raw or one-half cup cooked.

Because of their sugar content, the recommendation is for fewer fruits, but two to four servings are consistent with a healthy diet. A single serving would be one piece of fresh fruit, one-half cup of sliced or chopped fruit, one-fourth cup of dried fruit, or three-fourths cup of fruit juice. Be sure to choose a variety of fruits because each fruit offers different benefits. For example, citrus fruit is high in vitamin C, berries provide antioxidants, and bananas are rich in potassium. By choosing a variety of textures and colors, people will consume a variety of nutrients.

Breads, cereals, and pastas make up the largest group, with as many as eleven servings being recommended. Steer clear of the whites—white flour, white rice, white sugar. These all offer empty calories, raise blood sugar too quickly, and offer little to no nutritional benefits. Better choices include whole wheat breads, brown rice and other whole grains, and whole wheat pasta.

Eleven servings of grain may sound like a lot, but servings can add up fast. A single serving would include one slice of bread, one-fourth of a bagel, one-half of an English muffin, or three-fourths cup of cereal. Be sure to measure the cereal. For Americans, three-fourths cup of cereal may be a surprisingly small portion.

## Variety Is Key

A varied diet is key to a healthy lifestyle for anyone, but it is essential for a vegetarian. A good vegetarian diet relies on a rich and assorted blend of plant-based whole foods. Because children and teens are growing so rapidly, they are especially vulnerable to nutritional deficiencies if they have poor eating habits, so an assortment of healthy foods is important for them.

Christina Economos, a nutrition professor, directs the Tufts University Longitudinal Health Study on the lifestyle habits of young adults. Her research indicates that

kids who were most influenced by family diet and health values are eating healthy vegetarian or low-meat diets. But there is a whole group of students who decide to become vegetarians and do it in a poor way.... They eat more bread, cheese, and pastry products and load up on salad dressing. Their saturated-fat intake is no lower than red-meat eaters, and they are more likely to consume inadequate amounts of vitamin $B_{12}$ and protein. They may think they are healthier because they are some sort of vegetarian and they don't eat red meat, but in fact they may be less healthy.[34]

## Playing Hard to Get

Certain nutrients are more difficult for vegetarians to obtain. Without meat, vegetarians—especially women—have to work a little harder to get their iron needs met. Each month, women lose iron with their periods, and that iron must be replaced. An adult woman needs 18 milligrams of iron each day. An adult man needs 8 milligrams. Plant-based iron is harder to digest than animal-based iron. Good sources of plant-based iron include kidney beans (5.2 milligrams of iron per 1 cup serving), oatmeal (6.3 milligrams of iron per serving), cooked spinach (up to 6 milligrams of iron per serving), and tofu (6.6 milligrams of iron per serving).

If plant-based iron is combined with vitamin C, it is easier for the body to absorb. A spinach salad tossed with some cranberries or orange slices will provide a healthy dose of iron and vitamin C. Other sources of iron include dried beans, dried fruit (such as prunes, raisins, and figs), molasses, dark leafy greens, and cocoa. Cooking food, especially acidic foods, in an iron pot will also increase the food's iron levels.

If dairy products are not part of a vegetarian's diet, care must be taken to get enough calcium. Adults need 1,000 milligrams of calcium daily. Children, teens, and pregnant women or women who are breast-feeding have higher needs for calcium—up to 1,300 milligrams per day. A glass of milk contains 300 milligrams of calcium, and an ounce of hard cheese may have as much as 800 milligrams. A serving of tofu contains as much as 500 milligrams of calcium, and a half-cup of spinach has 150 milligrams. Maintaining good calcium intake is especially important for young people because the teen years are a time of significant bone building. Bone strength during the teen years is decisive in warding off osteoporosis in later years.

## Kinds of Vegetarians

In the United States four different types of vegetarians are recognized. Each group's main food source is plant-based foods, but each group also varies the diet slightly based on their beliefs.

# Why I Became a Vegetarian

"I became a vegetarian after I saw the movie *Fast Food Nation*. It showed the process of what they did to the animals, and I decided that I should not contribute to the immense amount of animal cruelty."
—Cheyanne L., age 16

"I didn't understand how you could justify not eating a person, but then justify eating an animal, because they both have the right to live."
—Matt S., age 15

"After I went to a local fast food restaurant, I had a burger that was undercooked and it made me sick. I decided that day that I wasn't going to eat red meat anymore."
—Brittney S., age 17

"I learned about vegetarianism from my family, they follow the same diet I do."
—Ray J., age 17

"I became vegetarian for health reasons. I was close to three hundred pounds and I was not feeling great. Me and a friend decided to see who could do it the longest and after a few months we both went vegan."
—Ted, age 19

## Lacto-Ovo Vegetarians

The lacto-ovo vegetarian is the most common type of vegetarian in America. It is also what people usually think of when they think of vegetarians. Lacto-ovo vegetarians eat milk and eggs in addition to a plant-based diet. This diet also makes it easier to get needed nutrients. And it makes it simpler to eat out, since many restaurants cater to this diet choice.

Like all vegetarian diets, plant-based foods need to be the emphasis. If a person loads up on too many eggs and dairy products and consumes too much fat, it is possible to face the same weight and health challenges as any nonvegetarian. By following the food pyramid guidelines, lacto-ovo vegetarians can enjoy a healthy diet and avoid overconsumption pitfalls.

## Lacto Vegetarians

*Lacto vegetarians abstain from eating eggs but can get the calcium they need from other dairy products, such as milk and yogurt.*

The lacto-vegetarian diet is the classic vegetarian diet of Hindus and Buddhists. Ancient religions followed this diet to assure they harmed no living thing. By monitoring their own milk intake to provide for a calf, they protected the health of both cow and calf. By refraining from eggs, they knew they would not accidentally eat a fertilized egg. For Hindus, eggs are considered "unclean."

Lacto vegetarians can easily obtain the calcium they need through milk, cheese, and yogurt. Protein needs, too, are easily met through either dairy products or plant-based protein sources. But as with the lacto-ovo vegetarians, too much fat can be a risk if lacto vegetarians do not monitor their dairy intake. Whether or not a person is a vegetarian, a cheese pizza and chocolate milkshake do not constitute a healthy meal. In addition to consuming too many calories, filling up on dairy will decrease the variety of other foods consumed. Like any vegetarian, it is important for lacto vegetarians to eat a wide variety of foods to ensure that they meet all their nutrient needs.

## Ovo Vegetarians

Ovo vegetarians, or "eggetarians," do not use milk products. Cows must have calves before giving milk, and those calves are produced, according to this group, for no other reason than to be slaughtered so their mothers can sustain the dairy industry. They contend that milk that should go to calves is being fed in mass quantities to humans. Eggs, on the other hand, do not need to be fertilized and are laid regularly. Consequently, no lives are lost when people eat eggs.

Because ovo vegetarians restrict their milk consumption, they must find a way to replace the calcium loss. Soy, rice, and almond milk products are on the market and are fortified with both calcium and vitamin D. Any of these products can be substituted for cow's milk for drinking and in most recipes. In most cases just substitute the same amount of the plant-based milk for cow's milk.

For growing children, teens, and pregnant women on this diet, calcium-fortified foods are helpful. Many cereals, juices, soy products, and other foods are now fortified with calcium. Some have both calcium and added vitamin D. These provide a convenient way to get the larger

> ## NUTRITION FACT
> ### 63
> Percentage of teens who go to their parents first when seeking information on health or nutrition.

*Although ovo vegetarians shy away from dairy products, they will eat eggs as long as they are from a free-range farm, which allows chickens the space to move around naturally.*

amounts of calcium these groups need. Other sources of calcium include leafy greens, broccoli, seaweed, and sesame seeds.

For many ovo vegetarians, an egg is not an egg unless it is "free range." Most supermarkets now sell free-range eggs. Free-range eggs come from farms that allow chickens to walk around.

Both brown and white eggs have the same nutritional levels. Different breeds of chicken simply lay different-colored eggs. Eggs contain 6 grams of high-quality protein along with zinc, vitamins A and B, iron, lutein, and choline, which is essential for fetal brain development.

An egg yolk also contains 210 milligrams of cholesterol. For some time, health professionals discouraged people from eating eggs because of this fact. Yet new research has shown that eggs do not raise cholesterol levels in most people. In fact, people can enjoy an egg each day, according to a Harvard study. In a 1999 study of 120,000 people, researchers found no link between daily eggs and diabetes. A similar Japanese study found no link between eggs and heart disease.

## Vegans

Vegans have the strictest diet of any vegetarians. Vegans eat only plant-based foods and shun both dairy and eggs. Many vegans do not eat honey, because they view this as an exploitation of honeybees. Vegans do not eat any animal-derived foods and will not wear leather. They are also careful not to buy any products with animal-derived ingredients such as gelatin.

Without nutrient-dense egg and dairy products, it can be difficult for vegans to get all the vitamins and minerals they need. Big plates of fiber-rich foods can fill a stomach before the body obtains all the nutrients it needs. If the empty calories in sweets and sodas are added to the mix, it can be impossible to fulfill nutritional needs.

A mainstay of a vegetarian diet, and essential to the vegan, is soy. Although relatively new to American diets, soy has been used in its many forms for more than three thousand years. Considered by some to be a wonder food, soy contains a complete protein, is rich in calcium, iron, and folate, and contains complex carbohydrates and omega-3, a healthy fat.

Traditionally soybeans were consumed in the form of tofu (soybean curd) and soy milk. Whole soybeans in the pod, known as edamame, are now widely available in U.S. grocery stores. Today soy protein is also used to make a number of meat substitutes. Soy burgers, soy hot dogs, soy "chicken," soy cheese, and soy yogurts are just a few of the soy-rich products available in local grocery stores. Additionally, many soy products are supplemented with essential vitamins and minerals that may be difficult to obtain for vegans and vegetarians alike.

# Eating Disorders

A recent study by the Vegetarian Resource Group showed that current and former vegetarians were at a higher risk for eating disorders than other groups. The study looked at more than twenty-five hundred males and females aged fifteen to twenty-three. Those people who identified themselves as current or former vegetarians were more likely to binge eat, use diet pills, purge, or use other extreme measures for weight loss.

This study follows a growing body of evidence showing that some people seeking vegetarianism are doing so because of an underlying eating disorder. The need to control eating habits fits nicely with the restricted diets of vegetarianism. Political and environmental philosophies associated with the label make vegetarianism a positive reason to restrict food. Unfortunately for some people, that control can simply be another step into a psychological disorder that can become life-threatening.

Vegetarianism can be a healthy lifestyle. But it can also be abused. Whether a person is a vegetarian or not, an eating disorder can be a serious problem and, if suspected, steps should be taken to seek help.

*Former and current vegetarians are at a higher risk for eating disorders than any other group. While vegetarianism can be a healthy lifestyle choice, it can also be abused.*

Vegans must also supplement their diets with vitamin $B_{12}$. Numerous studies have shown that most vegans have $B_{12}$ levels under the recommended thresholds. Vitamin $B_{12}$ deficiency can cause irreversible nerve damage. Since $B_{12}$ is found almost exclusively in animal products, vegans need to take a supplement to ensure they get adequate amounts.

Vitamin D, usually obtained from fortified cow's milk, is another nutrient that is difficult for vegans to acquire through food. Vitamin D is different from all other vitamins. It is the one vitamin that humans do not have to get from food. Humans can obtain vitamin D from sunshine, so a fifteen-minute walk in the daytime will provide ample vitamin D. If, however, sunshine is not in the forecast, a good supplement will be fine.

Iron and calcium can also be tricky nutrients for vegans. Vegans must pay more attention to be sure they are including fortified cereals and milks and a variety of nutrient-rich vegetables in their diets.

## Vegetarian Nutrition

So many different diets abound that it can be hard to know what to do. On the Mayo Clinic Web site, staff members address this problem when they compare all the different food pyramids to determine a healthy diet. They assess vegetarian, Asian, Latin American, Mediterranean, and their

*Vegetarian restaurants, such as this one in Connecticut, allow consumers to make healthy dietary choices away from home.*

own Mayo Clinic pyramids. All those pyramids have several things in common. According to the Mayo Clinic, they all state that people should:

- Eat more fruits, vegetables, and whole grains.
- Reduce intake of saturated fat, trans fat, and cholesterol.
- Limit sweets and salt.
- Drink alcoholic beverages in moderation, if at all.
- Control portion sizes and the total number of calories consumed.
- Include physical activity as part of a daily routine.[36]

Each of the vegetarian options described above meet or exceed the recommendations of the Mayo Clinic. Whether people choose to be lacto-ovo vegetarians, lacto vegetarians, ovo vegetarians, vegans, or simply to limit their intake of animal products, they can be assured that they are taking a step toward a healthier lifestyle.

# CHAPTER 4

# A Cultural Exchange

Many countries have long histories of vegetarianism or minimal meat consumption. Those diets can be based on religious, political, economic, or cultural reasons. In many cases the people of these countries enjoy better health and nutrition from these traditional diets. As the global community continues to expand, Americans can benefit from these imported diets.

## A Hindu Tradition

By far, the country with the most vegetarians is India. In India vegetarianism is deeply tied to historic religious beliefs. More than 80 percent of Indians are Hindu. Unlike other religions Hinduism cannot be traced back to one founder. Nor does it have a single holy book or one particular deity. Instead, Hindus may worship any of a thousand gods and goddesses. Those deities are thought to be the manifestation of Brahma, or the supreme soul.

Hindus believe that all souls reincarnate until they eventually reunite with Brahma. Depending on a soul's karma—the consequences of one's actions—a soul may be born into a higher or lower station. It will reincarnate until it eventually joins Brahma and finds release from the cycle of birth, death,

*Vegetarian choices abound at this Indian market. India is home to the most vegetarians in the world.*

and rebirth. Because Hindus believe that divinity inhabits all living beings, including humans and animals, they practice *ahimsa*, or nonviolence toward all living creatures. This belief in ahimsa is the basis for vegetarianism in the Hindu religion.

## A Changing Country

Despite this long tradition, today 60 percent of Indians are nonvegetarians. Overall, only 43 percent of religious Hindus and 28 percent of nonreligious Hindus practice vegetarianism. As non-Hindus enter India from other countries, some are also adopting the diet, including 8 percent of Christians and 3 percent of Muslims.

As a developing country, India is becoming a divided country. The rural poor are continuing to follow traditional lifestyles and eating patterns. Educated, urban Indians are obtaining good-paying jobs with multinational corporations. As is true in other developing countries, those urban Indians are becoming more Westernized, and that includes their eating habits.

India has become part of a growing trend among developing nations: Its consumption of meat (in this case, chicken) is rapidly increasing. While crop production has been rising at a rate of 1.5 to 2 percent per year, production of eggs and broiler chickens has increased at a rate of 8 to 10 percent annually.

The state of Gujarāt was considered one of the most vegetarian states in the country, with more than 70 percent of its residents practicing a vegetarian diet. Yet the changes in diet and food practices reflect the changing face of India today. According to the *Times of India*, a recent government report shows a 60 to 150 percent increase in production of fish, chicken, and eggs in Gujarāt.

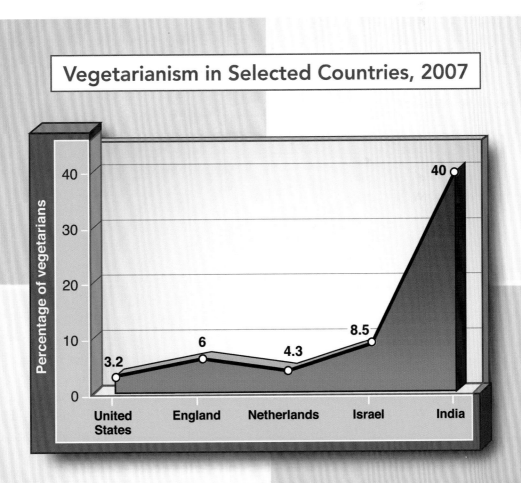

**Vegetarianism in Selected Countries, 2007**

Source: European Vegetarian Union, 2007. www.euroveg.eu/large/en/info/howmany.php; www.raw-food-health.net.

As the country becomes more developed, many people are moving away from traditional beliefs on eating and lifestyle. As they do, Indians are engaging in other habits that negatively affect their health. Thirty percent of rural young men now smoke. Coffee or tea is consumed by 96 percent of urban dwellers, and 13 percent of Indians drink alcohol. Urban jobs, while offering wages previously unheard of in India, are also inflicting enormous stress on workers. As Indians rapidly change their lifestyles, old health problems clash with new ones to create a difficult path for the country.

## Stuck in Two Worlds

India's rapid growth and changing diet is presenting two very different sets of problems. Srinath Reddy is the president of the Public Health Foundation of India. He says, "India's especially high rate of growth presents a challenge to our health. . . . In the U.S. . . . more moderate growth rates meant that the shift from 'shortage' based sickness such as malnutrition to such 'excess' based illnesses occurred slowly, with enough time for policy to catch up."[37] Growing at breakneck speed, India has not had the luxury of taking its time to catch up to the rapid changes.

Today diseases of extreme poverty such as malaria and malnutrition exist next to diseases of affluence such as diabetes and hypertension. Twenty-nine percent of the nation lives in poverty. Nearly 44 percent of India's children under age five face malnutrition. At the same time, more diabetics live in India than any other country in the world. Some estimates state as many as 50 million people in India suffer from the disease today.

Diabetes has followed India's modernization as it has in other developing nations. In fact, India's problems appear to be a microcosm of the world: According to the United Nations, the world now has more overweight than under-

**NUTRITION FACT**

28,773
Number of Chinese restaurants in the United States as of May 2010.

nourished people. Paul Zimmet, the director of the International Diabetes Institute in Melbourne, Australia, says, "I'm concerned for virtually every country where there's modernization going on, because of the diabetes that follows."[38]

With the largest vegetarian population in the world, India struggles with bleak statistics on health for both the affluent and impoverished. Abstention from meat alone cannot ensure health. Lack of adequate nutrition and calories plague India's poor. A fondness for sweets and high-calorie foods, coupled with a lack of exercise and lowered intake of plant-based foods, puts affluent Indians at risk for diabetes and other diseases of excess. The consequence of that impaired health is that, despite being vegetarian, an Indian's average life expectancy is only sixty-four years.

*Children suffering from malnutrition sit near their parents' work site in Gurgaon, India. Malnutrition is considered a disease of extreme poverty.*

# A World of Choices

Ethnic restaurants give vegetarians many opportunities to try new foods. Yet even the typical American diner has options for people choosing to go meatless.

**Italian:** Most tomato-based, oil-based, or even cream-based sauces will work (depending on what kind of vegetarian you are.) Pizza is also a natural choice. Couple pasta or pizza with a green salad for a balanced meal.

**Asian and Indian:** Any of these cultures offer a wide variety of vegetarian meals.

**Mexican:** Check to be sure food is not prepared with lard, which is a meat by-product. Black beans and rice, cheese enchiladas, chile rellenos, and nachos are all good choices for the vegetarian.

**Middle Eastern:** Hummus (chickpea spread) and falafel (a chickpea "meatball") can create salads, sandwiches, or main dishes. Match with a tossed green salad for a filling meal.

**American:** Salad bar, baked potatoes, sandwiches such as egg, cheese or PB&J, cheese sticks, and omelets are all widely available.

## Indian Food in America

Like food patterns in America, typical foods in India vary from region to region. Grains and legumes (especially red lentils) are both diet staples. Areas in the north use milk and yogurt products. Eastern areas rely on fish and rice. Spices such as cardamom, chili pepper, cumin, saffron, and turmeric are common.

Whereas some Indians are eating more like Americans, many Americans are eating more Indian food. They are choosing it for its exotic flavors and, with a little discrimination, for its healthy options. In America, Indian restaurants are common in urban areas in many regions. A 2007 study found that more than 1,200 new Indian food products had been introduced into the United States since 2000. Curries, lentils, and chai tea are all becoming commonplace choices. Indian products are found in both restaurants and supermarkets. Those new products reflect the growing interest in both ethnic and healthful food choices in the United States.

## Mediterranean Diet

Indian dietary habits may be ancient, but the Mediterranean diet is a modern label for the traditional dietary patterns of countries around that sea. By the 1990s scientists at Harvard School of Public Health, the World Health Organization, and the nonprofit group Oldways noticed that this diet produced remarkable health results. Chronic disease rates were some of the lowest in the world, and life expectancies were among the highest, even though medical services in the area were limited. In fact, the traditional eating habits of the region were so healthy, this group of

*Greek Orthodox monks look through a Mediterranean recipe book. The Mediterranean diet is one of the healthiest in the world.*

scientists declared the Mediterranean diet "the gold standard"[39] of eating patterns.

As they studied eating habits in the region, these scientists found several characteristics in common. An abundance of plant-based foods such as fruits, vegetables, nuts, cereals, and breads are the diet's base. Red meat is used sparingly, dairy use is low, and fish intake is moderate. The limited amounts of dairy products are usually fermented to create yogurt and cheese, with feta being the most commonly eaten cheese. Eggs are consumed no more than four times a week. Wine is drunk in moderate amounts, and olive oil is the major source of oil and fat. Legumes such as black beans, lentils, and garbanzo beans are frequently eaten. Fruit, especially fresh fruit, is usually eaten as a snack or dessert, with less-processed honey, not sugar, as an accompaniment. Unlike the American diet, the Mediterranean diet usually consists strictly of the three daily meals. Other than a bowl of fruit, snacking during the day is uncommon. Finally, the people in this region are very physically active.

Because dairy products and meat are like condiments—added for flavoring and not a main component of the diet—vegetarians can easily adapt this diet to their needs. With its rich mix of vegetables, grains, and legumes, requirements for vitamins and protein are easily met even when the token meat has been removed.

## A Heart-Healthy Diet

The Mediterranean diet is not a single diet. It is a mix of diets from peoples bordering the Mediterranean Sea. It is also not a vegetarian diet. Yet many vegetarians and nonvegetarians alike embrace portions of this diet for its healthful, whole-foods approach to eating. With its emphasis on keeping foods as natural and unprocessed as possible, the diet is rich in fiber and healthy antioxidants.

In 2001 the American Heart Association advised that the Mediterranean diet may be useful for the prevention and treatment of cardiovascular disease. Harvard researcher Walter Willett goes even further in discussing the diet's healthful properties. He says, "Our analyses suggest that healthy food choices that are consistent with the traditional Mediterranean diet, combined with regular physical activity and not smoking, can reduce the rate of heart disease by over 80%, stroke by 70%, and type 2 diabetes by 90%."[40]

The staff at the Mayo Clinic adds: "If you're looking for a heart-healthy eating plan, the Mediterranean diet might be right for you. The Mediterranean diet incorporates the basics of healthy eating—plus a splash of flavorful olive oil."[41] That flavorful splash of olive oil is the main dietary fat in the Mediterranean diet. Olive oil is a healthy fat. It is high in monounsaturated fatty acids, which are known to reduce blood pressure and lower cholesterol. Its antioxidants help prevent clogged arteries and lower the risk of cancer.

A European study published in the *New England Journal of Medicine* followed 22,000 people practicing the diet for four years. The closer people stayed to the diet, the less likely they were to die of either heart disease or cancer.

## Vegetarianism in Japan

For centuries the Japanese diet has been considered one of the healthiest in the world. The people of Okinawa in particular have been the subject of many studies and have inspired scientists with their large number of centenarians and vibrant health. And although scientists believe up to 50 percent of the Okinawans' long life can be attributed to "good genes," diet, they say, can make up the other half.

A history book written in the third century B.C. and titled *Gishi-wajin-den* detailed the beginnings of the traditional Japanese diet: "There are no cattle, no horses, no tigers, no leopards, no goats and no magpies in that land. The climate is mild and people over there eat fresh vegetables both in summer and in winter."[42] Several hundred years later, Buddhism spread through Japan. Today, of the citizens who claim a faith, 44 percent say they are Buddhist.

Founded on the teachings of Siddhārtha Gautama, Buddhism means "teachings of the Enlightened One." Gautama taught that by breaking the attachment to life and a sense of self, one could end the cycle of death and rebirth to reach enlightenment, or nirvana. Those who are reborn, Buddhists believe, will come back in some other form—human, divine, or animal—depending on their behavior in the last life. That connection to each other and the desire to cause no suffering is the basis of vegetarianism in Buddhism.

The traditional Japanese diet began to change in the last half of the twentieth century. After World War II the

## Coming to America

Miki Takekawa is a foreign-exchange student visiting from her native Japan. More than anything, sixteen-year-old Miki is surprised at the "big-ness" of food here. Miki says, "I was surprised at all the kinds—raspberry juice, cranberry juice, apple juice, and more. Nothing in my country is as large as here. Our grocery stores aren't so big; we don't buy so much. We buy one bag, maybe two—just what we need for today. Here, my host family buys many, many bags. There is so much food."

Unfortunately, that "big-ness" is rubbing off on Miki. Her friends told her she would gain weight on the American diet—and she has. Soft drinks, lemonade, and a lack of vegetables are all adding pounds as she eats like an American.

"It is hard," Miki says. "There is so much everywhere."

Miki Takekawa, interview with the author, November 1, 2009.

Japanese adopted America's eating patterns, and a serious increase in disease followed. When eating a traditional diet, only 1 percent of Japanese were obese, and only 1 to 5 percent of those over forty years old suffered from diabetes. But when they began eating a Westernized diet, diabetes rates shot up to 11 to 12 percent, and obesity climbed toward the American average of 30 percent.

*Japanese business-men enjoy a vegetarian meal in a Buddhist temple.*

## The Okinawans' Secret

The increase in disease made scientists go back and look at the Japanese diet. Good genes aside, they wanted to find out why the Okinawans lived so long. Several factors stood out, including calorie restriction, nutrients, and antioxidants.

Calorie restriction is one of the main reasons the Okinawans live so long. Okinawans eat 25 percent fewer calories than other Japanese. But the high levels of nutrients and antioxidants in the food they do eat may also contribute to the nonexistence of dementia, cardiovascular disease, and cancer among Okinawans. They obtain their nutrients from numerous different sources.

One source is cruciferous vegetables. Okinawans consume five times the amount of cabbage, broccoli, brussels sprouts, kale, cauliflower, radishes, watercress, and parsnips than Americans eat. Another dietary source is shiitake mushrooms. Used as a medicine for more than six thousand years, these mushrooms are loaded with powerful antioxidants and are known for their ability to enhance the immune system and lower cholesterol. Seaweed is high in iodine and minerals. Both nori (from cold waters) and kombu (from warm waters) are a regular part of the Okinawan diet.

Tofu, a staple of the Japanese diet, has been shown to lower cholesterol and improve cardiovascular function. It is a good source of protein and is packed with nutrients. Green tea, another staple, has been linked to reduced cancer risk. Green tea also has been shown to lower blood pressure and cholesterol and help with stroke and heart disease. Lastly, the Japanese consume more than 154 pounds of fish (70kg) per person per year. Fish is rich in essential fatty acids that contribute to good health.

Although fish is on the Okinawans' plates, vegetarians can easily modify this diet and adopt the other components of this healthy lifestyle. With their high population of people over one hundred years old, the Okinawans are clearly doing something right.

## An American Embrace

Americans are flocking to Japanese cuisine. As they move past eating sushi in restaurants, Americans are now buying products for their own pantries. A sampling of U.S. sales figures for 1996 and 2006 shows this trend. In 1996 Americans bought nearly $6.2 million worth of kamaboko (fish cake),

but by 2006 that figure had increased to more than $21 million. Rice vinegar sales nearly doubled, and green tea sales increased sixfold as Americans sought out this healthy and flavorful cuisine.

As with the Okinawan diet, small modifications can make the Japanese diet a healthy choice for vegetarians. Replacing fish with tofu or tempeh is an easy alteration. Rice, sea vegetables, and other fruits and vegetables inherent in the cuisine provide a varied and healthy option for those people wanting to embrace the distinctive flavors of this culture without consuming meat or fish.

*Japanese restaurants, which were not so common in the mid-twentieth century, are gaining popularity in the United States.*

## China's Dilemma

Like the Japanese diet, the traditional Chinese diet, which is built on grains, vegetables, and legumes, is easily adapted to a vegetarian diet. Chinese cuisine includes generous amounts of dark leafy greens, including romaine lettuce, watercress, bok choy (white-stemmed cabbage), kai choy (mustard cabbage), and Chinese kale.

Yet like India, as China develops a modern economy, its consumption of meat is skyrocketing. More than half of all Chinese come from low-income and rural households that obtain more than three-fourths of their calories from grains. Although the consumption of a wide variety of proteins, including dog and even fungus-infected caterpillars, has been a Chinese tradition, meat has always been an infrequent luxury to a large segment of the population.

This is changing. Even in rural homes, nearly 7.7 pounds (3.5kg) of poultry are now eaten in the poorest households annually. (For comparison, the average American eats 90.6 pounds [41.09kg] of poultry annually.)

But as China's economy changes, people in the middle and upper classes are changing their diets rapidly. In 2008 China's people consumed an additional 39,938 million tons (36,231 metric tons) of beef compared with 1995. Much of that beef is eaten at fast food restaurants or is purchased from Western-style supermarkets, with supermarket purchases doubling between 1999 and 2005. As for many emerging nations, America's economy and customs represent the model to be copied in China, and meat consumption is a hallmark of America's affluence.

## Urban Diseases

As their diet changes, however, developed-country maladies plague the Chinese. For example, according to CBS News, the number of breast cancer cases in China's richest cities has risen 37 percent in the past ten years.

In addition, whether America exports its diet to China or immigrants adopt it when they arrive in this country does not matter. According to a study conducted by the Keck School of Medicine at the University of California–Los Angeles, when Asians leave their traditional diets, illness follows. Although the study did not comment on other health issues affecting Asian immigrants to the United States, such as smoking and exercise, this multigenerational study showed that the more they ate like Americans, the

*The proliferation of American fast food restaurants, such as this McDonald's in Beijing, China, contributes to Asians leaving their traditional diets and adopting American eating patterns.*

higher their risk for cardiovascular disease. In addition, a study conducted by Stanford University found that Chinese immigrants who adopted a typical American diet were four to seven times more likely to develop colorectal cancer than those who remained in China.

## Reaching for Authentic Cuisine

Americans, on the other hand, are asking for authentic Chinese food and adapting recipes to include healthy choices in their diets. Chinese restaurants have been in America for more than a hundred years. More Chinese restaurants exist in America than any other ethnic restaurant. But the

Chinese food served in America looks nothing like native Chinese food. Americanized Chinese food has more fat, more meat, and more syrupy sauces than authentic Chinese food. However, as Americans seek healthier food choices, they are beginning to ask for more authentic Chinese ingredients and less of the sweet, fat-laden fare of the past.

Stir-fry vegetables are available pre-chopped and packaged in most produce sections, and bags of mixed bok choy, snow peas, and broccoli can be found in the frozen food sections of many markets. Fresh-cut vegetables quickly prepared in a wok and served over brown rice are appearing in restaurant chains around the country.

## Cross-Cultural Lessons

Vegetarian diets are as different as the region or culture they come from. Whereas both the Japanese and Indian diets can be vegetarian, the healthful aspects of these diets are dramatically different when Indians give in to their famous sweet tooth and fat consumption. It is also true that diet—whether vegetarian or not—is not the only factor in a person's overall health. Exercise, smoking, drinking, stress, and income are also factors that affect the health of any individual regardless of diet.

Yet certain facts hold true worldwide. High-calorie, high-fat, processed-food diets bring with them a plethora of health problems. Low-fat, plant-rich diets, with or without small amounts of lean meat, appear to be the healthiest choice for people regardless of culture.

# CHAPTER 5

# Getting Started

Vegetarianism is more like a journey than a destination. Getting started on that journey simply requires the desire to do so. Like any journey, vegetarianism is a road with smooth places and obstacles as well as many small decisions along the way. As Americans embrace the vegetarian diet, choices become easier as products and services become more available. Whether vegetarianism becomes a new lifestyle or a place to visit, the health benefits of a diet rich in plant-based nutrition can be rewarding.

## Making the Decision

Becoming vegetarian is a decision as individual as the person making it. Whatever decision is made and however the decision is made, it is important to note that it is a personal decision. Both political and moral vegetarians move toward the decision for reasons of justice and a desire to improve the world. Respect for differing food choices is another way to increase the justice on the planet and improve personal relations.

Whether a person simply takes a step closer to a plant-based diet or embraces it with open arms, the nutrients of all those fruits and vegetables will be an asset to his or her health.

## Dinner Dynamics

If the entire family is not practicing vegetarianism, a cooperative approach can satisfy everyone. Sharing cooking duties is one way to make a family member's transition to a new diet easier on everyone. Mutual consideration also helps. Is the family eating spaghetti and meatballs? Just serve the meatballs on the side, and let family members add them to meatless spaghetti sauce at will. Is that casserole just not the same without cheese? When it is finished, scoop out a corner for the vegetarian, then sprinkle cheese on the rest. It will melt in a few minutes outside the oven, or pop it back in for that crusty top.

All it takes is a little thought and planning. With a small amount of effort, families can honor the vegetarian of the group and still provide for their own needs.

## How to Begin

The journey into a new lifestyle begins with the first step. In the case of vegetarianism, that means assessing the current situation. Three easy steps will start a person on the path to a healthier lifestyle.

First, make a list of current vegetarian meals—families may already be enjoying a number of vegetarian meals. Start with what is familiar. Use five pages to create a list, and label each page with one of these five headings: Breakfast, Lunch, Dinner, Snacks/Desserts, and Eating Out. Brainstorm with family members to list all the meals that are currently vegetarian.

Second, list meals that could be vegetarian with just a small alteration. Can marinara sauce replace meat sauce in spaghetti? Will soy crumbles work in the chili? How about a vegetable base in soups, rather than meat broth? Let the family work together so that everyone feels involved and honored. Try to make it fun. Know that some substitutions will work and some may not turn out. Finding the humor in the disasters helps ease tensions and furthers a desire to experiment.

Third, decide on one or two changes in diet. Do not overdo it. If a family eats meat every night of the week, quitting

"cold turkey" is going to make everyone feel deprived. In that case one or two vegetarian nights are a big change. Most people wean themselves off animal protein by cutting out red meat, then poultry, and finally fish. If they are going vegan, eggs and finally dairy products complete the transition. This method is not set in stone. Let people find a method that works for them.

When the list is complete, families may be surprised at how many of their eating habits are already compatible with a vegetarian diet.

*Families can work together to help make the switch to vegetarian meals by making simple substitutions in their existing diets.*

## Meatless Meals

Especially in the beginning, meat analogues—soy products produced to look and taste similar to meat or chicken—are an easy way to adjust a favorite recipe. These products are

# A Sample Day

Many Web sites offer ideas for sample meals. These daily meal plans are not set in stone, but instead are intended to provide ideas for creating a balanced diet. Two days' worth of menu ideas are below.

## Day 1
**Breakfast:** Bagel with apple butter, banana, calcium-fortified orange juice.

**Lunch:** Black bean and corn burrito with guacamole, lettuce and tomato; a side of rice; tortilla chips and salsa; soy milk.

**Dinner:** Spaghetti with marinara sauce; broccoli, zucchini, yellow squash, mushroom, cucumber, and carrot salad; soy milk.

**Snacks:** Hummus and baby carrots, fruit smoothie, protein bar.

## Day 2
**Breakfast:** Whole-grain cereal with banana and soy milk, calcium-fortified orange juice.

**Lunch:** Baked beans with soy hot dog; leafy green salad with tomatoes, broccoli, carrots, and cucumbers; whole grain roll; soy milk.

**Dinner:** Tofu-vegetable-cashew stir-fry (tofu, broccoli, cabbage, carrots, onions, snap peas, celery, and garlic with stir-fry or teriyaki sauce and sprinkled with cashews), rice, fruit kabobs.

**Snacks:** Fruit smoothie, power bars, multigrain or black bean chips with tofu dip.

often found in the vegetable section or the freezer section of the supermarket. Here's a simple substitute for a classic American dish:

**Chili sin Carne (Chili Without Meat)**
1 8-ounce package soy crumbles
2 tablespoons olive oil
1 30-ounce can red kidney beans, rinsed and drained
2 14.5-ounce cans Italian-style diced tomatoes
1 package chili flavoring mix

Heat the oil in a heavy saucepan. Add the soy crumbles and break apart with a spoon as they cook. Add tomatoes, chili mix, and beans (rinsing and draining canned beans helps cut down on their gas-producing side effects). Heat until bubbly. Serve with corn bread.

For more meatless recipes, log on to the Internet. Key words such as "meatless," or "vegetarian" in front of, for example, "meatloaf recipe," will yield a wide variety of options. Tailor recipes for family tastes. Add bell peppers or omit the garlic from the recipe to make it feel familiar. If tofu is being used as a meat replacement, increase the spices in the dish, because tofu brings virtually no taste of its own. As the journey becomes more comfortable, very different-tasting recipes can be added.

## Other Substitutions

For vegetarians who do not eat dairy or eggs, some recipes will need modifications. Luckily, plenty of choices are out there that make such substitutions simple and tasty.

There are many options to replace eggs in recipes. Try experimenting with favorite recipes to find which alternative best suits each dish. Some commercial egg substitutes are vegetarian friendly. Other alternatives to eggs in a recipe include mashed bananas, applesauce, pureed prunes or carrots, soy milk, or yogurt.

*Noodle manufacturers learn about using liquid eggs as a substitute for shell eggs in Singapore. Some egg substitutes are vegetarian friendly.*

As a rule of thumb, pureed prunes have a richer, heavier flavor than eggs and are good in foods such as vegetable meatloaf, brownies, and chocolate or spice cakes. Applesauce and soy milk affect the taste of recipes the least. Finally, bananas lend nice moisture to recipes.

Replace butter with a vegetarian-friendly margarine spread or with bananas or applesauce. Substitutes for cow's milk include soy, rice, or almond milk products. Several milk substitutes on the market are fortified with both calcium and vitamin D. In most cases just substitute the same amount of plant-based milk for cow's milk.

## A Packed Pantry

A vegetarian's pantry may look a little different than the typical American pantry. But by stocking some basics, people will have the flexibility to create nutritious and delicious meals without much trouble. Several of these basic foods are listed below.

**Legumes:** Pinto, kidney, black, cannellini, garbanzos (also called chickpeas,) peas, and lentils are good basic beans. All provide an excellent source of fiber and protein.

**Pasta:** Choose a variety of shapes for both eye appeal and interesting textures. Aim for whole-grain pasta. Many on the market today taste nearly identical to their white-flour cousins yet pack substantially more nutrition. Experiment with different brands.

**Grains:** Barley, bulgur, couscous, a variety of rices, quinoa, and wild rice will add variety to dishes. Brown rice is tasty, but maybe some nights the chewy texture of bulgur will crunch better or the nutty flavor of wild rice will enhance the dish.

**Canned goods:** Pinto, black, kidney, and vegetarian refried beans make for quick burritos or chili dishes. Stewed tomatoes (many varieties are available with garlic, basil, chilis, or other tasty additions) can be thrown over pasta, spread over bread, or dumped into soups and chilis. Pineapple, mandarin oranges, or applesauce make handy fruits for salads, whereas stewed prunes and baby-food jars of prunes, carrots, and applesauce are good additions for

## Throw-Togethers

Dinner does not have to be a major undertaking. Use the table below to throw together a quick and easy main dish. Just take one item from each column to mix and match in your own masterpiece. Serve with a big green salad and some whole wheat bread.

| Sauté any one of the following in a large skillet using olive or canola oil. | Add any one of the following to create a sauce. | Add these uncooked into the sauce, cover and simmer 30 to 40 minutes. |
|---|---|---|
| Soy crumbles and onions | 1 jar marinara sauce plus ½ jar water | 8 ounces uncooked penne pasta |
| Sliced zucchini and crushed garlic | 2 cans diced tomatoes plus ½ can water or red wine | 8 ounces uncooked rigatoni |
| Firm crumbled tofu and chopped bell peppers | 1 jar mushroom-flavored spaghetti sauce plus ½ jar water | 1½ cups barley |
| Chopped broccoli and spinach | 2 cans cream of mushroom soup with 2 cans water | 8 ounces uncooked elbow macaroni |
| 1 package soy "chicken" strips and onions | 3 cups water and 1 tablespoon vegetable-flavored bullion with 2 tablespoons Italian seasoning | 1½ cups brown or brown and wild rice |

baking. Garlic and pesto come in glass jars in the produce section of the grocery store. These can be stored in the cupboard until opened, but then must be placed in the refrigerator. They are good, already-prepared ways to add flavor and nutrients to a variety of dishes.

**Oils and spices:** Olive and canola oils are standards for cooking, baking, and adding atop salads. But sesame, walnut, macadamia nut, and grape seed oils all add unique flavors to a variety of foods. Farmer's markets and many health food stores also carry bulk spices in drawers or large jars. People can buy a tablespoon or so of a new spice or spice mixture and try out a new flavor without incurring a big expense. It is a good way to play with new tastes.

**Sauces:** Soy, stir-fry, peanut, spaghetti, pizza, barbeque, and pasta sauces, as well as salad dressings and a variety of vinegars, will add pizzazz to any dish. Rice vinegar has a light, low-acid taste that works well with fruits and cabbage. Balsamic vinegar has a rich, earthy taste that is great on grilled Portobello mushrooms or grain salads.

**Sweeteners:** Some vegetarians shy away from honey because, like milk and eggs, it requires intensive services from the animal kingdom. Sugar and brown sugar are fine, but other sweeteners are healthier and add interesting flavors. Some examples are real maple syrup, blackstrap molasses (a by-product of sugar manufacturing), or agave syrup, which is made from cactus.

Below is a good recipe that can go from the pantry to the bowl in about an hour. The surprising pop of sweetness will even appeal to those who usually do not like lentils.

**Straight-from-the-Pantry Lentil Soup**
2 cups lentils
10 cups water
2 tablespoons Italian seasoning
Garlic salt to taste
1 tablespoon chopped garlic (from the jar)
1 14.5-ounce can stewed, chopped tomatoes with basil
   and onion
½ cup blackstrap molasses (or to taste)

Rinse and sort lentils, checking for foreign matter. Put lentils, water, garlic, and Italian seasoning in a saucepan, bring to a boil, then lower to a simmer. Simmer for about forty minutes or until lentils are tender. Add stewed tomatoes and molasses, and heat through. (As an option, this soup is great with chopped onions, celery, carrots, peppers, zucchini, or other vegetables. Just add them at the start.) Serve with crusty bread and green salad.

## Filling the Fridge

By keeping a well-stocked refrigerator, new vegetarians will not be tempted to grab junk food or run to the local fast food restaurant. A well-stocked refrigerator includes plenty of the following items.

**Vegetables:** Do not buy too many fresh vegetables at once or they will spoil. But keep a nice variety of choices in the crisper. Cut up carrots, celery, broccoli, radishes, and other veggies for a quick snack with hummus, salsa, or dip. Pre-packaged stir-fry, coleslaw, and grated carrot mixes are quick and easy ways to throw together a fast meal when there is no time for chopping.

**Fruits:** Keep a variety of fruits on hand, both for snacking and as part of daily meals. Apples with almond, soy, or peanut butter make an easy, nutritious snack. Roll a banana in chopped nuts and pop it in the freezer for a vitamin-packed "popsicle." Add apples and pears to curry, pineapple to stir-fry, and kiwi or oranges to a green salad.

**Nuts and seeds:** Nuts are best stored in the refrigerator. Their oils can turn rancid if stored in the cupboard. Walnuts, cashews, sunflower seeds, pumpkin seeds, almonds, hazelnuts, and soy nuts are just a few of the wonderful varieties available today.

**Dairy:** Milk and yogurt or enriched soy, rice, or almond milk and soy yogurt are essentials for their versatility.

## NUTRITION FACT

Before modern hygiene, vegetarians got their needed $B_{12}$ vitamins from the dirt, bugs, and waste left on the vegetables they pulled from the ground.

*Keeping a well-stocked refrigerator full of delicious vegetarian food can help prevent unhealthy eating.*

Chocolate soy milk, although not necessarily a staple, also provides a wonderful, sweet treat. Butter or margarine, mayonnaise or soy mayonnaise, and eggs or an egg substitute round out the dairy section.

**Fast-from-the-fridge lunch:** Top yogurt with a variety of fruits and a tablespoon of nuts. Add a piece of whole wheat toast with red pepper hummus to round out the meal.

A well-stocked pantry and fridge will provide all the ingredients needed to create a wondrous array of tasty meals and snacks. Adventure is the key. Do not be afraid to experiment. One of those creations may just be the next big sensation.

## Venturing Out

Leaving the safety of a well-set-up vegetarian kitchen can feel challenging. Whether it is the school cafeteria, a restaurant, a friend's home, or a traditional family gathering, the key to success is integrity.

In a cafeteria or restaurant, communication is the vital to finding foods that suit a vegetarian lifestyle. Restaurants are designed to serve patrons. There are too many other choices out there for restaurants to ignore the needs of their guests—those guests can just go somewhere else. But a restaurant cannot know how to help if no one asks, so ask. Very often a simple change can make many entrees vegetarian friendly. Can they leave the chicken out of the stir-fry? Can they serve the Cobb salad without the meat?

Asking might even open up some new adventures. In-and-Out Burger, a restaurant chain in the western United States, has a "secret" menu for vegetarians. Although it is not publicized, vegetarians can get a grilled cheese sandwich and other vegetarian-friendly choices simply by asking. Other restaurants have similar options that may not appear on the menu.

School cafeterias also tend to be vegetarian friendly. Most offer at least one vegetarian option for students. Peanut butter and jelly is the old standby. Yogurt, salads, and bags of fruit and nuts are often options as well.

Family gatherings can present some challenges. Traditions die hard, and, if everyone has always loved Grandma's turkey, she might be offended when it is suddenly taboo for one or more family members. Planning ahead is the best defense. It is not fair to let Grandma slave away at a meal only to have her efforts rejected without warning. If she knows well in advance that dietary habits have changed, she can have time to adjust.

Betty Rowe has been making a traditional turkey dinner for as long as her family can remember. Recently, her grandson called to tell her he could not eat turkey this year. She says: "There were so many things to eat—we just left the turkey out for him. By the time you're a grandma, you've learned how to make lots of substitutions for all your grand-kids' changing needs."[43]

In most cases families also like to accommodate their children's friends. Cheryl Doe says: "Just tell me. I really want my kids' friends to feel welcome at our house. I have no problem preparing meatless meals if I know ahead of time."[44]

## Journeying Past Fast Food

For the vegetarian and nonvegetarian alike, fast food can be a minefield. While not a good option for healthy eating, people may occasionally find themselves in a fast food restaurant. It is important to be able to make the healthiest choices possible when eating there. Healthy choices require a little investigation.

With fast food it is best to be cautious. In an effort to make cheap yet tasty food, corporations take some unusual steps to flavor their products. In one fast food chain, the fries and hash browns are flavored with beef flavoring. The salad dressings have ground anchovies. The cookies are made with honey and the special sauce with egg yolks. In another the bagels are made with L-cysteine that is derived from duck feathers. Several Web sites provide a list of truly vegetarian foods available in fast food restaurants. One of those sites is listed in the "For More Information" section of this book. By clicking on a particular chain, the viewer can get a product-by-product list of acceptable foods.

Whereas avoiding meat-based foods in fast food places is one solution, avoiding fast food restaurants altogether is another. It may be fun to visit a fast food place occasionally with friends, but all people, not just vegetarians, would improve their health by finding different ways to eat and socialize. Try a "free the fridge" night. Have people get together, share their culinary skills, and see what they can create from what is already in the refrigerator and pantry. Or have a "pool party" where people pool their money to make an awesome veggie pizza or zesty soup.

*Preparing dinner with friends and family can be a fun, healthy option for vegetarians.*

For centuries humankind has socialized around communal meals. Societies have shared their bounty and created meals and memories together. It is only in the last few decades that the fast food movement has changed the way people eat and socialize. Today people can choose a different way.

## Choosing a Path

After all the research is accomplished and the soul-searching is done, each person must decide what is right for him or her. People make life decisions for a variety of reasons. No

*The second annual Veggie Pride Parade in New York City, where participants voice concern about the effect that eating animals has on the environment.*

one answer is right for everyone. By educating themselves about vegetarianism in particular and a healthful lifestyle in general, people can take a positive and mature step toward a better life.

Whether the choice to be a vegetarian is based on nutritional, political, or moral reasons, or whether someone simply wants to consume more plant-based foods, the journey toward the vegetarian lifestyle is a journey into a healthful, nutritious pattern of eating. With a little planning and education, people can make good choices about their diet and lifestyle.

# NOTES

## Chapter 1: A Growing Trend

1. Sydney, interview with the author, November 12, 2009.
2. Quoted in Bio-Medicine, "Vegetarianism: An Antidote to Obesity," April 3, 2006. www.bio-med icine.org/medicine-news/Vegetari anism-3A-An-Antidote-To-Obesity -9004-1.
3. Miranda Hitti, "Vegetarian Diet May Help Weight Loss," WebMD, April 3, 2006. www.webmd.com/ diet/news/20060403/vegetarian -diet-may-help-weight-loss.
4. KidsHealth, "Vegetarianism: Older Vegetarians and Teens," The Nemours Foundation, 2010. http:// kidshealth.org/parent/nutrition _fit/nutrition/vegetarianism .html#a_Older_Vegetarian_Kids _and_Teens.
5. Vegetarian Resource Group, "How Many Vegetarians Are There?" May 21, 2003. www.vrg.org/journal /vj2003issue3/vj2003issue3poll .htm.
6. Steven, interview with the author, November 12, 2009.
7. Quoted in Richard Corliss, "Should We All Be Vegetarians?" *Time*, July 2002. www.time.com/time/covers /1101020715/story.html.
8. Quoted in Associated Press, "Are You a 'Flexitarian'? Meat-Eating Vegetarians Transform the Movement," MSNBC, March 16, 2004. www.msnbc.msn.com/id/4541605.
9. Quoted in Associated Press, "Are You a 'Flexitarian'?"
10. Quoted in Mary Brophy Marcus, "More Young People Go the Vegetarian Route," *USA Today*, November 15, 2007. www.usatoday.com /news/health/2007-10-14-veggie- kids_N.htm.
11. Elisabeth, interview with the author, November 11, 2009.
12. Quoted in Associated Press, "Are You a 'Flexitarian'?"
13. Vegetarian and Meat-Free Group, "The Product," 2010. www.meat- free.org.uk/mf_product_intro .aspx.
14. Vegetarian Resource Group, "The Market for Vegetarian Foods," 2009. www.vrg.org/nutshell/market .htm#market.

## Chapter 2: Why Turn to Vegetarianism?

15. Frank, interview with the author, November 12, 2009.

16. Quoted in Maggie Fox, "Even America's Youth Have Clogged Arteries," Rense.com, July 26, 2000. http://dailynews.yahoo.com/h/nm/20000725/sc/heart_cholesterol_dc_1.html.

17. Quoted in Fox, "Even America's Youth Have Clogged Arteries."

18. Quoted in R. Morgan Griffin, "Cholesterol-Lowering Foods: Tasty, Functional Foods Help You Lower Cholesterol Naturally," WebMD, February 2, 2009. www.webmd.com/cholesterol-management/guide/cholesterol-lowering-foods?print=.

19. Griffin, "Cholesterol-Lowering Foods."

20. Neal D. Barnard et al., "A Low-Fat Vegan Diet Improves Glycemic Control and Cardiovascular Risk Factors in a Randomized Clinical Trial in Individuals with Type 2 Diabetes," Diabetes Care, American Diabetes Association, 2006. http://care.diabetesjournals.org/content/29/8/1777.full.

21. Internet Health Library, "Heart Disease Research: Alternative & Complementary Therapies," December 5, 2006. www.internethealthlibrary.com/Health-problems/Heart%20Disease%20-%20researchAltTherapies.htm.

22. Quoted in Internet Health Library, "Cancer Research: Alternative & Complementary Therapies: Vegetarianism and Cancer," December 4, 2006. www.internethealthlibrary.com/Health-problems/Cancer%20-%20researchAltTherapies.htm.

23. William Harris, "Cancer and the Vegetarian Diet," Vegsource, December 21, 1999. www.vegsource.com/harris/cancer_vegdiet.htm.

24. Candace, interview with the author, November 11, 2009.

25. Brittney, interview with author, November 11, 2009.

26. Quoted in Vegetarian Times, "Why Go Veg?" www.vegetariantimes.com/resources/why_go_veg.

27. Elisabeth, interview.

28. Jennifer M. Fitzenberger, "Dairies Gear Up for Fight over Air," Fresno (CA) Bee, August 2, 2005, p. 22.

29. Lierre Keith, The Vegetarian Myth. Crescent City, CA: Flashpoint, 2009, p. 1.

30. Quoted in CNN Interactive, "Oprah Accused of Whipping Up Anti-beef 'Lynch Mob,'" Cable News Network, January 21, 1998. www.cnn.com/US/9801/21/oprah.beef.

31. Keith, The Vegetarian Myth, p. 3.

32. Quoted in International Vegetarian Union, "The Moral Basis of Vegetarianism," August 3, 2006. http://ivu.org/news/evu/other/gandhi2.html.

33. Humane Society of the United States, "Humane Eating," 2010. www.humanesociety.org/issues/eating.

## Chapter 3: Nutritionally Speaking

34. Quoted in Corliss, "Should We All Be Vegetarians?

35. Matt, interview with the author, November 11, 2009.

36. Mayo Clinic, "Food Pyramid: An Option for Better Eating." www.mayoclinic.com/health/healthy-diet/NU00190.

## Chapter 4: A Cultural Exchange

37. Quoted in Nandan Milekani, *Imagining India*. New York: Penguin, 2009, p. 367.
38. Quoted in N.R. Kleinfield, "Modern Ways Open India's Doors to Diabetes," *New York Times*, September 12, 2006. www.nytimes.com/2006/09/13/world/asia/13diabetes.html.
39. Oldways, "The Traditional Mediterranean Diet," Oldways Preservation Trust. www.oldwayspt.org/traditional-mediterranean-diet.

40. Quoted in John Edward Swartzberg, "Greek Lessons," *UC Berkeley Wellness Letter*, June 2009, p. 2.
41. Mayo Clinic, "Mediterranean Diet: Choose This Heart-Healthy Diet Option." www.mayoclinic.com/health/mediterranean-diet/CL00011.
42. Quoted in Mitsuru Kakimoto, "Vegetarianism and Vegetarians in Japan," *IVU News*, 1998. www.ivu.org/news/3-98/japan1.html.

## Chapter 5: Getting Started

43. Betty Rowe, telephone interview with the author, November 12, 2009.
44. Cheryl Doe, interview with the author, November 11, 2009.

**ahimsa:** Nonviolence toward all living things.

**calorie:** A measurement of the amount of energy a food provides.

**carbohydrates:** One of the substances in foods that provide energy. Carbohydrates are made of carbon, oxygen, and hydrogen.

**centenarian:** A person who lives to be one hundred years old.

**fat:** An oily substance found in the body tissue of animals and some plants. Fats are used for energy and are stored to keep the body warm.

**minerals:** Any inorganic elements (calcium, iron, potassium) that are obtained from food and are essential for the functioning of the human body.

**obese:** Usually defined as being 20 percent over ideal body weight.

**overweight:** Up to 19 percent heavier than ideal body weight.

**protein:** A substance found in plant and animal cells. Foods such as cheese, eggs, and beans are sources of dietary protein.

**sustainability:** A method of harvesting or using resources so that the resources are not depleted or permanently damaged.

**vitamin:** One of the substances in food that is necessary for good health.

## Compassion over Killing (COK)

PO Box 9773
Washington, DC 20016
phone: (301) 891-2458
e-mail: info@cok.net
Web site: www.cok.net

The COK's mission is to end abuse and cruelty in agricultural animals. This group promotes vegetarianism as a way to build a kinder world.

## EarthSave

PO Box 96
New York, NY 10108
phone: (800) 362-3648
e-mail: info@earthsave.org
Web site: www.earthsave.org

EarthSave strives to educate people that their food choices have a major effect on their health, the environment, the planet, and all life on the planet.

## Green People

41 Highland Ave., Suite 206
Highland Park, NJ 08904
Web site: http://greenpeople.org

Green People provides a large directory of environmentally friendly businesses as well as products, including dog food, clothing, and beauty supplies.

## Organic Consumers Association (OCA)

6771 S. Silver Hill Dr.
Finland, MN 55603

phone: (218) 226-4164
Web site: www.organicconsumers.org

The OCA is a political action group whose goal is to educate the public on all green issues. Videos on vanishing bees, political commentary, directories to buy green, and tips on buying organic foods are all included on the site.

## The Vegetarian Resource Group (VRG)

PO Box 1463
Baltimore, MD 21203
phone: (410) 366-8343
e-mail: vrg@vrg.org
Web site: http://vrg.org

The VRG has recipes and articles especially for teens and a section for vegans. The group produces a journal and online brochures, which may be downloaded for free. The VRG offers scholarships to young vegetarians.

# FOR MORE INFORMATION

## Books

Lierre Keith, *The Vegetarian Myth*. Crescent City, CA: Flashpoint, 2009. A former vegan, Keith compiles impressive data as to why vegetarianism does not accomplish what it hopes to accomplish, either nutritionally or environmentally.

Debra Halperin Poneman and Emily Anderson Green, *What, No Meat? What to Do When Your Kid Becomes a Vegetarian*. Toronto: ECW, 2003. Although written for parents, this is an excellent resource for the whole family. In a calm and reassuring manner, the authors lay out for parents the benefits of vegetarianism. Family recipes are also included.

Eric Schlosser, *Fast Food Nation*. New York: HarperPerennial, 2004. A *New York Times* best seller, this is the book that inspired the movie and exposed the dark side of the all-American meal.

Stefanie Iris Weiss, *Everything You Need to Know About Being a Vegan*. New York: Rosen, 2000. Focusing on vegans, this book offers an argument for the lifestyle along with a sampling of recipes.

## Films

*Babe*, DVD. Directed by Chris Noon. 1995; Universal City, CA: Universal Studios, 2003. This story of an extraordinary pig led many people to seek vegetarianism—including Babe's costars.

*Chicken Run*. Directed by Nick Park and Peter Lord, 2000. Glendale, CA: DreamWorks Animation. This funny fantasy film is based on serious, real-life issues as Rocky Rooster and Georgia Hen try to escape their horrible living conditions and their ultimate death on a factory farm.

*Food Inc*. Directed by Robert Kenner. 2008; New York: Magnolia Home Entertainment, 2009. This film chronicles the impact of America's corn production policy on all aspects of agriculture, both here and around the world.

*Super Size Me*. Directed by Morgan Spurlock. 2003; Culver City, CA: Sony Pictures, 2004. Thirty days of nothing but fast food does some real health damage to the lead character while opening the eyes of viewers to America's unhealthy eating habits.

## Web Sites

**E: The Environmental Magazine** (http://emagazine.com). *E: The Environmental Magazine* is an award-winning online magazine promoting political action for green causes. This magazine offers articles, advice, political alerts, and calls to action.

**EcoBusinessLinks** (http://ecobusiness links.com). This is a directory of ecologically friendly businesses. Under dozens of headings, users can find eco-friendly grocers, electronics stores, or car dealers.

**FarmersMarket** (www.farmersmarket .com). This site provides a directory of local farmers' markets. Follow the simple directions on the site, type in a zip code, and the directory will locate the nearest market.

**Happy Cow** (www.happycow.net). This Web site lists restaurants, famous vegetarians, recipes, political groups, communities, and organizations supporting the vegetarian lifestyle.

**Savvy Vegetarian** (www.savvyvegetarian .com). This site offers recipes, coaching, blogs, articles, and general information on how to maintain a vegetarian lifestyle.

**Vegetarian-Restaurants** (www.vegetar ian-restaurants.net/OtherInfo/Fast FoodRest.htm). This site lists most major fast food chains. By clicking on the chain's name, viewers can access a list of foods that are vegetarian friendly, along with information on unexpected meat-based ingredients.

# INDEX

# PICTURE CREDITS

## ABOUT THE AUTHOR

Award-winning author Susan M. Traugh has been writing children's books and curricula for over twenty years. A former teacher, Traugh holds an MA in education specializing in curriculum development. In addition to writing, she currently teaches workshops and seminars for educators. She lives in California with her husband and three teenagers.